How Burnout Stops:
A Practical Guide to Stress Management,
Burnout Prevention and Burnout Recovery

David Thorpe

www.coolout.co

First published in 2023 by David Thorpe
South Australia, Australia

ISBN 9780648520979

Contents

Introduction

Speaking from personal experience, I know burnout is not fun. It makes us feel mentally and physically exhausted, leaving us drained. Just thinking about our work can fill us with dread, and even anxiety, as we wonder about the next source of stress.

My personal experiences of burnout

I first remember experiencing burnout during the completion of my Master thesis. I was one year into the two-year allowed time. In comparison to the experiences of other students, I had supervisors who were not as supportive of me. Additionally, I had a strong, driving desire to write the best thesis in history. These primary factors resulted in symptoms during that time, including insomnia, poor decision-making, and an overall sense of mental exhaustion, which ultimately affected my academic performance at that point in my candidature. My burnout relief only came in the knowledge that there was a clear end in sight to the situation. Other supervisors and faculty assured me that my feelings were completely "normal" and commonly experienced by higher-degree candidates and that most just "got over it". At the time, this all struck me as strange. I could not agree that these feelings and experiences should have been considered normal and dismissed. Still, I did not know of any solutions to help myself or other fellow students I knew were experiencing burnout around me.

My second experience of burnout occurred in a workplace where there was a misalignment of values between the employees and a manager, which resulted in nearly all the employees under that manager leaving the organisation within a few months. Interestingly, it wasn't exhaustion that I felt when faced with the stressors caused by this manager's actions; rather, it was a feeling of ineffectiveness and cynicism toward my work. The other employees and I felt we could not do the excellent work that clients were expecting from us because of this manager's guidance.

During these burnout experiences, the big question for me was determining who was to blame. Was it all my fault, driven by my personal pursuits of success and unwillingness or inability to deal with the barriers to that success? Or were there systematic issues within the organisations that produced barriers? Did I need to try and ignore the issues and improve my yoga poses, or let leadership know every issue every day in the hope that the stressors would disappear? Alternatively, was the only solution to leave the organisation and try again, hoping the same barriers wouldn't reappear at the next organisation? Below those questions, I had a fundamental question; How do I make my burnout stop?

My journey started towards finding the answer.

Who is this book for?

This book is intended for anyone who suspects they may be experiencing burnout. It is also for anyone who suspects someone they know is experiencing burnout and wants to know how to help them. Furthermore, this book is for organisational leaders who want a useful resource to help them address and solve potentially burnout-causing and stress-inducing issues that arise for their stakeholders as they do their work. When referring to 'work' in this book, I'm talking about any context of work you are involved in, including careers, family responsibilities, caring duties, volunteering, and everything in between. Burnout can be experienced by anyone, regardless of what they do.

Throughout this book, there is the underlying thesis that, to stop burnout, we need to understand stress and burnout causes within both the environment (typically an organisation, hence the frequent use of the term 'organisation', but maybe the nature of the work, such as being a carer) and the individual. Strategies and tools will be proposed for overcoming these causes at both the organisation and individual levels. Some resources swing one way or the other. Some place the full blame of stress on the individual, offering solutions such as yoga and mindfulness without considering that the environmental stressors may be too strong and deeply rooted

3

to be overcome by individual strategies alone. Other resources significantly focus on the organisation and suggest that a shift in the mission statement, values, or workplace culture will be enough to combat a burnt-out workforce, without considering that some individuals will remain susceptible to burnout regardless of the workplace culture due to their inner beliefs.

That is why, in the best of worlds, this book is intended for both the organisation and the individual to work through together. Yes, getting everyone on board is much easier said than done, but it is in this joint effort that burnout is least likely to persist, with individuals and organisations working together towards reducing and mitigating stressors.

What's in this book?

As I'm sure you're aware, the advice comes thick and fast when one begins a journey into understanding stress and burnout. Like many psychological disorders and experiences, burnout is a subject of extensive research and ongoing debate. Even the concept of burnout is subject to disagreements and multiple definitions, depending on the resources you explore. This book aims to be as practical as possible, only commenting on these debates when necessary.

Instead, this book offers practical advice and strategies based on the latest understandings of stress and burnout. It discusses what individuals and organisations can do to help stop the experience of burnout and prevent it from returning. While brevity was a deliberate aim in producing this book, further resources will be suggested for if any specific area piques your interest.

You will also encounter stories throughout this book. Some stories are fictional illustrations of strategies, while others are based on real-life experiences of individuals and organisations working through burnout. To protect the anonymity of individuals and organisations, names have been changed.

Will this book be helpful?

I would like to establish a few expectations from the outset of your engagement with this book:

1. There is no standardised, one-size-fits-all solution for burnout. Solutions to burnout should directly address the specific causes of stress and burnout. The severity and consequence of a stressor will vary between individuals, so we need to be mindful not to invalidate people's experiences. What may be a mild annoyance to one person could cause panic attacks in another. Therefore, as you read through this book, learn the principles and determine which stressors are most relevant to your situation. Then, you also need to determine which strategies may be the most suitable steps towards recovery. This leads to the second point of setting expectations.

2. No self-help book is a replacement for getting professional and qualified personal advice when it comes to mental health. As will be discussed, burnout is often recognised as a comorbidity of other mental health issues, such as clinical depression and clinical anxiety. Addressing these conditions is outside the scope of this book. The focus of this book is limited to the discussion of stressors not caused by chronic mental health or physical health issues.

Here is the good news

There are real solutions to the problem of burnout, and you can begin making changes within the hour to help you better cope with stressors. Burnout does not have to be a permanent part of your life. It does not need to be an issue that stops you from doing what you love most.

As discussed earlier and further explored throughout the rest of the book, this is How Burnout Stops:

1. Reducing environmental stressors.

2. Reducing individuals' susceptibility to stressors.

I hope this book provides helpful and practical solutions, validating those of you experiencing stress and burnout and guiding you down a clear path towards experiencing engagement, well-being, and fulfilment in your life.

David Thorpe
June 2023

Chapter 1:
How Can We Define Burnout?

There are two primary concepts I want to discuss in this first chapter:

1. What burnout is.
2. What burnout is not.

This ensures we are on the same page when we later discuss strategies for stopping burnout. Of course, we need to know exactly what we aim to stop. Equally importantly, we must put boundaries around our burnout discussion due to common burnout comorbidities beyond this book's scope. At the end of this chapter, we'll also briefly touch on why we should aim towards stopping burnout in the first place, both from individual and organisational perspectives. But first, let's meet Paula.

Paula's work kept her up at night

Paula: wife to Oscar, mum of two adult children, and business manager for a small charitable organisation. That summed up her daily life. She didn't have any 'technical' burnout vocabulary to describe how she felt, yet she constantly felt under pressure, a feeling she knew couldn't be normal.

She attributed the pressure she felt at work to her own expectations of good performance. Every week, she needed to wrangle enough volunteers to have the required resources for the weekly events her charity put on for those in need. She would have trouble falling asleep the night before each event, worried that the volunteers would not turn up. She felt a lack of volunteers would not only make her look bad in front of the people she was trying to help but also be a reflection on her abilities to keep reliable volunteers on the rosters.

Early in her career with the organisation, she had felt a wave of disappointment each time a volunteer ceased to continue. She wondered if she could have done something different to keep them on. But then it kept happening, volunteers leaving without much warning, and she didn't feel she could stop it. Her struggles felt insignificant to the 'real' struggles of the people her organisation was serving, and this feeling prevented her from addressing her own stress.

She had heard people around her, even on her staff, say things like, "I feel stressed out" and "I feel burned out," but she didn't really understand when or where these terms could be used or if someone could self-diagnose themselves with 'burnout'. Over the years, she had heard people in her organisation complain about cumbersome tasks, demanding managers, or irritable clients—real "problems" with tangible "causes"—. Still, she couldn't identify the tangible cause of her own feelings. She could see other people in similar roles with similar problems at other organisations who seemed, for lack of a better word, "happy" about their work. That's what she wanted.

Did Paula have burnout?

What is burnout?

I wish I could just state, "Burnout is X," and leave it at that, but unfortunately, it is not that simple. There is even disagreement over the spelling of the word: Burnout? Burn-out? Burn out? Definitions can significantly differ between sources, so we must create a clear context for this book's discussion. Parker, Tavella and Eyers spend much of a whole book defining burnout, concluding that it can be best defined by its symptoms .

We may define burnout as a response to an individual's chronic stressors. For those of you who believe you might be experiencing burnout, I hope you find this validating: If you have a persistent negative reaction to a stressor in your life, you are likely experiencing burnout. Paula's insomnia and anxieties were her responses to the stressor of depending on volunteers to fulfil her assigned task and the responsibility of hosting the weekly charity event. We can therefore propose that Paula was experiencing burnout.

Also, we should note that burnout can refer to responses to stressors in any life situation, not just occupations, as suggested by some definitions (e.g., International

Classification of Diseases (ICD-11)). Many have experienced burnout due to unique stressors from caregiving, strenuous family relationships, or even volunteer roles. Although much of this book discusses burnout in the context of occupational roles and tasks, the stressors and strategies discussed can often be applied to non-occupational situations.

We've established burnout is a response to stressors. What are stressors? Again, we will sidestep the debatable and diverse definitions of 'stress' and suggest that a stressor is something signalling danger or requiring action. This definition allows us to explore why stressor reactions might differ from person to person. When Paula experiences symptoms from the stressor of not having enough volunteers, she is likely feeling a threat of danger—danger to her role and reputation as a successful charity business manager. In contrast, Harold, a business manager at a rival charity, faces the same stressor but sleeps soundly at night. He is aware that he will need to start making a marketing plan to recruit more volunteers the next day, but he doesn't perceive the stressor as any danger. Charities lose volunteers all the time.

Many other examples of stressors are discussed in part two of this book, but here are a few:

- Short deadlines for tasks.
- Managers who constantly change their minds.
- Demanding clients or patients.
- Unrealistic expectations of work performance from managers.
- Threats of funding reductions or even getting fired.

- Regular contact with traumatic situations or trauma-affected people.

What is stressful in any of these examples and causes burnout in one person might be nothing more than a call to action for another and then be forgotten after being added to a future to-do list. That is why it is important not to invalidate or criticise someone experiencing burnout. What might seem like a mere annoyance to you might feel literally life-threatening to someone else. These differences likely result from individual temperaments, beliefs, and unique life experiences.

Again, part two provides many examples of reactions individuals might have to stressors, but here are a few:

- Emotional or physical exhaustion.
- Cynicism about the effectiveness of work.
- Apathy about work results.
- Lack of empathy or care about clients or fellow workers.
- Inability to focus on tasks.
- Inability to make decisions about tasks.
- Impulsivity and irritability towards others.

Just as stressors can cause varying degrees of responses, the actual response can also differ. We need to be careful not to jump to conclusions just because of the presence or absence of a specific burnout symptom.

What burnout is not

Burnout is not a one-off reaction to a single instance of stress. We might suggest that Paula's initial disappointment when volunteers stopped participating was not an experience of burnout but undoubtedly still a stressful situation. Yes, she may have lost sleep that night, reflecting on why the volunteer left and even anxious over the future of her events. But, the next day, she might have taken comfort and felt relief when she could see other reliable volunteers still committed to the events, and her insomnia and anxiety symptoms ceased. But when the next volunteer left...and the next one...and the next one...her insomnia and anxiety became a daily occurrence, seemingly without an end in sight. She felt it was exhausting. Every day she came home drained and unmotivated to continue her work. Her relationship with her husband suffered as her thoughts were constantly on work and the challenges she anticipated for the next day.

Burnout is not just another term for depression or anxiety. These psychological disorders might coexist with burnout, but addressing stressors and burnout symptoms in a person experiencing clinical depression will not necessarily make the depression subside, and the same goes for anxiety. Treating these disorders might reduce one's susceptibility to burnout, but suggesting treatments for these disorders is beyond this book's scope. Depression can be misidentified as burnout when only burnout has been tested for, and that is why it is very important to consider any family history or symptoms of depression if burnout recovery strategies seem ineffective. Symptoms of depression can include:

- Unattributable causes or stressors causing a feeling of sadness.
- Suicidal thoughts.
- Inability to be cheered up or distracted.
- Notable changes in appetite and weight.

- Loss of ability to feel pleasure.

If any of these symptoms are present, individuals should seek the help of a qualified psychology professional for diagnosis and assistance.

It is also important to note that the causality of comorbidity has not been definitively established. For example, burnout might lead to clinical depression or anxiety . This information is not meant to instil anxiety but to emphasise the importance of not assuming burnout symptoms will simply disappear without being addressed. Individuals should seek help as soon as any stressors or symptoms begin to feel more than what they can handle on their own.

Burnout is also not just another term for exhaustion. Stressors can create an exhausting environment full of pressures, demands, and calls to action, requiring more time and focus than one has to offer. But if relief from exhaustion comes when the given project or task finishes or after a period of rest, it is unlikely to be an experience of burnout. However, if you return to work after a period of rest, are filled with a sense of dread, and feel exhausted before the day's end, you might be experiencing burnout. Exhaustion, whether mental, physical, or emotional, is the most mentioned symptom of burnout in definitions. If someone experiences exhaustion that does not cease, even after reasonable rest, this might be evidence to consider more focused burnout recovery interventions.

A final note on this topic: Ultimately, it is not the responsibility of a manager or friend to shut down someone if they have expressed that they feel they are experiencing burnout. Instead, this should be the start of a judgement-free conversation focusing on identifying stressors and planning prevention, mitigation, or recovery strategies.

Why should individuals address burnout?

From the individual's perspective, the answer to why they would want to address burnout is straightforward: experiencing burnout hinders a person from reaching their full potential due to the stressors acting as barriers that prevent them from performing or achieving to the best of their ability.

An individual experiencing burnout is looking for positive well-being; they seek to experience satisfaction and fulfilment in their tasks, roles, responsibilities, and work/life balance. How those broad experiences manifest will differ from person to person. Individuals have varying values, goals, and expectations for what they want their lives to look like, as well as unique stressors that require personalised attention and solutions. Combatting burnout for the individual involves addressing issues that obstruct the individual from achieving a life that aligns with their values, goals, and expectations.

It can be very hard for someone to vulnerably open up about what they believe is causing burnout in their life. If Paula were to try and describe her stressors to Harold, it is natural she might start self-criticising: 'This really isn't such a bad situation. There's no reason I should be experiencing burnout. You have to deal with the same stuff. The people we help have to deal with much worse.'

Conversely, saying, "I know how you feel; I went through similar...," to someone who has shared their burnout experiences can potentially be invalidating, given the unique and varying factors causing their stress. More importantly, be mindful not to criticise or invalidate the individual by saying things like, "Chin up. You've got a great job. Just take a deep breath and keep going. It won't last forever!" Individuals don't want to address burnout merely to swat away a nuisance. Their stressors can feel life-threatening.

We address burnout because it isn't a necessary part of any individual's experience. There is no evidence to suggest that experiencing burnout is an essential aspect of any work or life scenario. Burnout is also not a badge of honour.

Why should organisations address burnout?

This is one of the more complex burnout questions. Why should organisations invest resources, including time, money, and energy, into preventing burnout?

One can make an anecdotal argument for the economic benefits of reducing the prevalence of burnout in the organisation. I'm sure we all know someone who had to leave their job because "I was just completely burned out." However, we cannot make a blanket statement that investing in burnout prevention will necessarily reduce turnover rates. This is because burnout is driven by multiple factors, some of which are beyond the control of the organisation and are dependent on the individuals' temperament, beliefs, unique life experiences and other external factors, such as sociocultural changes that may contribute to burnout. There is, however, a risk of increased turnover when systematic stressors within an organisation are not acknowledged or remedied.

Another economic argument is that having a burned-out workforce can lead to lower-quality outputs and reduced organisational effectiveness. This is due to burnout symptoms such as stakeholders' sense of ineffectiveness, problems with focusing, and impaired decision-making. Essentially, even when burnout does not result in an organisation losing personnel, the quality of those personnel resources may deteriorate.

If an economic argument for addressing burnout is not persuasive enough, please consider the argument in the preceding section Why should individuals address burnout—but let's frame it in the context of an organisation: Organisations should address burnout because it does not have to be a condition that they inflict upon their stakeholders. There is no evidence to suggest that causing burnout is a necessity of your organisational systems.

What's in the rest of this book?

The rest of this book will elaborate on the idea that burnout is ongoing symptoms arising from stressors. To prevent burnout, we must mitigate or reduce the individual's exposure and susceptibility to stressors. To recover from burnout, we must use strategies to help individuals overcome their symptoms. To stop burnout, we must address stressors rooted in both the individual and the organisation.

The rest of part one of this book continues to provide foundational, practically relevant information on stress and burnout for individuals and organisations. Again, this book was not created to discuss academic, theoretical debates around burnout. We do not yet have a complete understanding of stress and burnout, but from what we do know, we can certainly identify specific causes of burnout and stress and start putting strategies into place to prevent those stressors from continuing to affect people.

In Chapter 2, we'll look at different perspectives of burnout causes, focusing on the contexts of individual and organisational stressors. This is followed by examining different signs, symptoms and responses individuals may have to the stressors.

Chapter 3 will discuss known burnout prevention strategies, considering what both the individual and organisation can do. Thankfully, most stressors have relatively straightforward, easy-to-understand prevention strategies. However, putting these in place requires continual attention from the individuals and commitment from all stakeholders to make changes at the organisational level.

In Chapter 4, we will explore burnout recovery remedies for individuals who are already experiencing burnout. We'll consider both short-term solutions and strategies that look to help in long-term recovery. There is no single, one-size-fits-all solution, nor is there a solution known to last forever. However, there are adaptable strategies suitable for the ever-changing landscape of work and life.

In Chapter 5, we will detail the organisation's response to burnout and what stakeholders can do to implement burnout prevention strategies, help others overcome burnout, and create a workplace that minimises psychosocial risks. We offer checklists for the busy manager and further suggestions for those enthusiastic about improving the organisation's outputs and the stakeholders' lives.

Lastly, in Chapter 6, we will provide some goals for individuals and organisations to aim for. When you're in the midst of stress and burnout, it can be difficult to identify what the effective or stress-free functioning of a person or organisation looks like.

Part two of this book is structured as a reference guide. Again, while there is no one-size-fits-all solution to burnout, there are commonly recurring stressors in organisations and people's lives, common burnout symptoms and reactions to these stressors, and consequently, a range of prevention and recovery strategies that can be recommended. This guide discusses nearly one hundred examples of stressors and provides relevant recommendations for both individuals and organisations that could help reduce the prevalence and effects of these stressors. This list is intended not to be exhaustive but to initiate a conversation between affected parties about addressing burnout.

Chapter 1 in 100ish words

- Burnout is a reaction to an individual's chronic stressors.
- Stopping burnout requires the combined effort of both individuals and organisations.
- Burnout is not just another term for depression, anxiety, or exhaustion. It is not the role of others to dismiss an individual's experience of burnout; rather, it should start a conversation about identifying stressors and implementing mitigation strategies.
- Individuals should address burnout because experiencing burnout is not inevitable, regardless of their circumstances.
- Organisations should address burnout to reduce the risk of low-quality outputs and compromised organisational effectiveness.

Chapter 2:
What causes burnout?

This chapter aims to discuss how people end up experiencing burnout. Firstly, it must be said that, theoretically, anyone can experience burnout in their lives. This is due to the understanding that multiple factors can cause burnout. In this chapter, we will examine who is more likely to experience burnout and what some of the signs and symptoms are in those experiencing burnout. To begin with, let's meet Jonathon.

Jonathon's group project

Jonathon, 22, was in the final semester of his three-year undergraduate business degree. He wasn't sure exactly what he wanted to do for a long-term career, but he considered the possibility of pursuing a research degree quite exciting. He recently discovered that to do honours (a prerequisite for a PhD), he needed to achieve at least a 5.0 GPA, which most students generally considered an 'easy' grade. At that point, he was sitting at 4.75. He calculated he could reach 5.0 if he achieved High Distinctions in his four remaining subjects. He felt confident in three of the subjects, but one subject, Accounting II, was making him feel physically ill. The subject required him to complete a group-work assignment, and his group was, in his own words, "absolutely ridiculous". Initially, the groups were randomly assigned. Jonathon felt like his fate had been left up to chance. After their first group meeting, when he recognised the others were putting in the least effort possible, he went to the course coordinator and expressed his concerns. "Her response was something like 'Tough luck. You can't choose whom you work with in the real world'," Jonathon said. He felt that the course coordinator wasn't offering him any support. Jonathon worried that this group assignment could be the single thing that would prevent him from continuing towards a research degree.

When asked how the stress was affecting him, he said it made him anxious about his future. He also felt cynical about whether the university actually cared about him. He suggested that he was feeling resentment, not only towards the other group members but also towards the course coordinator. He was anxious about the potential of doing the entire group assignment by himself and was feeling mentally exhausted from dwelling on the issue every day for the last couple of weeks.

Perspectives of burnout causes

When considering burnout, along with many psychological phenomena, the answer to "What is the cause?" depends on perspective. In the context of burnout, one might potentially examine the individual level, the interpersonal level, the organisational level, and the societal level. That is, burnout may be caused or exacerbated by an individual's physiological or psychological factors, including temperament, beliefs, and unique life experiences. Factors contributing to burnout can also include interpersonal relationships, organisational system issues, and stressors resulting from societal expectations or norms. As you can imagine, these four perspectives can be mixed and matched, depending on one's approach. Given that this book aims to be as practical as possible, the focus will be on stressors for which there are practical solutions to mitigate causes.

Let's briefly discuss societal expectations or norms. Jonathon faced a social expectation in his university degree that he should achieve at least a 5.0 GPA. This social expectation reinforced his personal belief that to be considered successful enough, he needed to meet that mark. Individuals who care for impaired family members may perceive a social norm that they are the 24/7 carers for that family member, regardless of the stress this causes compared to employing help. Every culture, career, and setting have some social norms that can exert pressure on the individual. As you can imagine, societal expectations and norms are challenging for the individual to control and overcome. The strategies for preventing and managing societal burnout stressors practically need to be discussed in the context of what the individual can do to be less susceptible to these stressors.

An interpersonal perspective on burnout suggests that life is a series of relationships, and when there is a lack of reciprocity in a relationship, there is a strong chance of burnout. Jonathon perceived his relationship with his group members as essentially non-existent in terms of reciprocity, and he received no support from his course coordinator when that was what he expected from the relationship. When interpersonal relationships contribute to burnout, whether familial, social or work relationships, overcoming them requires both parties to be willing to come together. This is difficult because it is often the case that the two people have opposing and often conflicting goals. This book is not about relationship management, but there are individual strategies, to be discussed, that people can use to have productive discussions about stressors caused by others.

The organisational and individual perspectives on burnout will be discussed in their respective sections below, as they are the focus of this book due to the practical strategies that an organisation and an individual can implement to mitigate burnout causes.

Organisational perspective: Which organisations are more likely to experience burnout?

The organisational perspective on burnout stems from the traditional view that burnout is a solely occupational phenomenon, suggesting that burnout results from organisational systems that impose demands on individuals exceeding the individual's available resources. Resources here may refer to the individual's time, mental and physical energy, focus, effort, or skills, to name a few. This perspective also suggests that certain occupations demand more resources than others and are likely to deplete an individual's resources faster.

The occupations in which workers are most likely to experience burnout are often summarised as those involving frequent interpersonal interactions, often called 'helping' occupations. These include healthcare and medical professions, teachers, counsellors, and clergy. Why are workers in these occupations most likely to experience burnout? From the organisational perspective, it would suggest that interpersonal interactions are resource intensive. One might argue that this is due to these jobs involving the unpredictable nature of dealing with other people. It is natural for people to prioritise their own needs above others. This is especially true in helping sectors, where people in need are unlikely to reciprocate or give anything back to the helper. Such interactions tend to be very much a one-way relationship and, therefore, can be draining for the helper. Additionally, the helper is likely to feel a sense of responsibility for caring for the person. This sense of responsibility can also be very exhausting, especially when frequent, time-sensitive decision-making is required.

Other sectors where burnout is high include those involving interaction with traumatic content, such as helping professions and emergency services. Exposure to traumatic content is largely unavoidable in occupations in these sectors, so it is especially important that organisations have systems in place to reduce psychosocial risks, including frequent stakeholder engagement, traumatic content control measures, and minimisation of necessary exposure to the content.

There are, moreover, some occupations that are more likely to attract high-performing professionals where, from the individual perspective that will be discussed in the following section, their personality types and beliefs about their performance may increase the likelihood of burnout in these occupations.

To conclude, just because an individual is not working in one of the above occupations does not mean they are safe from burnout. Any occupation, role or organisation has the potential to demand more resources than the individual can provide. In addition to examining the stressors that can stem from organisational roles, tasks, and responsibilities, we also need to discuss which individual factors may contribute to the increased likelihood of burnout experiences.

Individual perspective: Which people are more likely to experience burnout?

There is a lack of evidence suggesting that an individual's demographics strongly cause burnout. Some studies have identified women as having a higher likelihood, but there is no real consensus on the relationship between age and burnout. Other demographics, such as education, where relationships to burnout have been identified, can be explained by the fact that highly educated people are more likely to pursue a professional career where, as discussed in the previous section, burnout is more prevalent.

Rather than relying on demographics to explain burnout, a more fruitful path is to examine the personalities of individuals to understand who is most likely to experience burnout. Evidence suggests that people with a Type A personality are more likely to experience burnout. People with a Type A personality tend to be driven towards achievement and feel a sense of urgency, impatience, and competitiveness to get there. We can infer why this personality type is more likely to lead to burnout: when one is driven towards achievements, barriers that prevent the individual from reaching that achievement are likely to quickly become stressful situations.

It's important to remember that these achievements are likely set by the individual. Yes, some organisational goals may be set for the individual to achieve, but the individual still chooses to take on these achievements. Frequently, people with a Type A personality often extend their achievement goals for themselves in one way or another, including self-regulated time or quality goals. For Jonathon, this goal was a high GPA. No one intrinsically set this goal for him. The group project presented a potential barrier to reaching the level of success that he had set for himself.

Of course, as with all discussions of personality types, it needs to be taken with a grain of salt since personalities can be situation specific. An individual may have a Type A personality at work, or even just within a domain of their work, but not at home or in their personal life.

Another way to consider the individual perspective of burnout is to identify which people are least likely to experience it:

1. Those who don't care about the outcomes of their work. When people see their occupation as just a job, and barriers arise to them doing their job, they might even welcome the barrier as an excuse not to be responsible for the job's outcome.

2. Those who don't care about other people. If you don't care what anyone else thinks, feels, or is affected by the outcomes of your job, you're unlikely to experience burnout.

If those blasé descriptions of people above, of which I'm sure we all know one or two, made you feel repulsed, and it is my opinion they should, then you will be happy to know there is a middle ground of reduced susceptibility to experiencing burnout without becoming apathetic about the outcomes of your work or sociopathic about your relationship to the people around you.

Let's return to the main question "What causes burnout?" by providing a layman's answer of "stress upon the individual". Stress upon the individual, in turn, is caused by factors in the individual's environment, which can be a life event or stimulus that the individual perceives as threatening. This suggests the individual perspective of burnout is the one that requires the most attention.

It must be highlighted that a situation stressful to one person may not necessarily be stressful to the next person. This could mean that a given stressor may cause one person to eventually experience burnout, but the same stressor may not necessarily cause their colleague to experience burnout. Unbeknownst to Jonathon, one of his fellow students in his group may have also perceived the lack of group cooperation as threatening to his grades but does not see it as a threat to his livelihood. We need to be mindful not to invalidate a person's feelings of burnout just because the people around them experiencing the same situation are not showing symptoms of burnout.

A situation or stimulus does not necessarily need to be a chronic stressor to cause burnout. It might have been just one really bad experience, but for it to be burnout, it is generally recognised that the symptoms need to be ongoing. One highly stressful, emotionally charged meeting between a boss and an employee may be enough for the employee to fill their thoughts with anxieties of termination, leading to emotional exhaustion and their work becoming less effective due to being distracted by their anxiety.

What are the signs of burnout?

As with any abnormal psychological experience, signs and symptoms of burnout can vary greatly from person to person. In line with the aim of this book, it's beyond the scope to enter into a long discussion as to where an individual's psychological experience sits on a spectrum. Instead of stating, "You need to identify a certain number of symptoms to conclude that one is experiencing burnout, " I suggest that any signs or symptoms can indicate that a person is experiencing burnout.

In this section, I'll suggest some top-level, observable patterns of an individual's behaviour that may be signs there are further internal symptoms of burnout. As we will address further in Chapter 3, if an individual shows any signs of changes from their known normal patterns, it's perfectly valid to check in with the person and ask how they are to gain more information on what is causing the symptoms.

Changes in the individual's usual patterns of work outputs

These changes may be a reduction in the quality/quantity of the worker's outputs due to the individual's distraction from their work or even a cognitive impairment due to exhaustion. These changes could even be an increase in the quality/ quantity of the worker's outputs, induced by the worker spending extra time and resources on creating the outputs. Ineffectiveness is not necessarily a symptom of burnout.

An increased amount of time requested off

Without wishing to state the obvious, if a worker is asking for more and more time off, it may be an indication that they are feeling less invested in their work. Alternatively, the worker may be suffering from physiological symptoms related to stress and tiredness that genuinely make them sick. If a worker is asking for frequent time off at the last minute, it may be worth checking in with them.

An increased quantity of complaints

People make complaints when they perceive there to be issues. When someone has an issue, it can often be that the surface issue is not necessarily the real, core issue they want to be dealt with. For example, a worker may make complaints about their heavy workload, where the real issue is they feel their manager is not consulting them on their capacity when tasks are being assigned. These complaints may be made between workers when it is perceived that management is unwilling or available to listen or respond to complaints. This is why it is important that organisations have a culture of listening and responding to workers. That means leadership uses resources to hear what the worker has to say and respond through words or actions that communicate to the workers that they have been heard.

Decreased quantity of communication

When a worker is experiencing burnout, they may begin to shut in and communicate less with others about how they are feeling. This can either come from a place of fear of inadequacy or heightened apathy that management will actually do anything about the stressors in the environment.

What are the symptoms of burnout?

Here, we discuss some high-prevalence symptoms a person feeling burnout may experience. To date, there is not a definitive list of burnout symptoms. Part 2 of this book discusses many more symptoms in specific contexts, but the following symptoms have been identified as being commonly associated with burnout.

Emotional exhaustion

This is probably the most frequently associated symptom with people who have experienced burnout. It could be caused by the individual being constantly preoccupied with the stressful situation or stimulus and unable to come up with a resolution for how to proceed away from the stressor. This can be exemplified by people who cannot turn off at the end of the day or compartmentalise between work and life. Other associated descriptors with emotional exhaustion can be feeling overwhelmed, emotionally drained, and easily distracted from what the individual desires to focus on.

Physical exhaustion

Physical exhaustion, and physiological sicknesses, can be symptoms of burnout. This can be due to sleep being interrupted by thought preoccupation or the individual not regulating their work-life balance. This can be a vicious cycle where physical exhaustion leads to poor health decision-making, which leads to more physical exhaustion.

Cynicism

As a result of exhaustion, or sometimes even as a protection from thinking, people who are experiencing burnout may become highly cynical of their work and those they work with. They may be cynical that their work has meaningful outputs or that the stressful situation will change. They may become highly apathetic about that work, and this can lead to increased absence from work and the individual putting in less effort.

Anxiety

Experiencing burnout may lead to anxiety. The individual may not be sure about what the future holds if they continue in the stressful environment or even what would happen if they tried to relieve themselves from the stress or symptoms. Some individuals may feel anxious about how others will view their personal identity if they fail or change. Other individuals may feel anxious about their personal finances or career in general if their stressor caused them to need to leave the stressful situation.

Depression

Experiencing burnout may also lead to individuals experiencing depression. There are different types of depression, and environmental stressors may cause non-melancholic depression. As outlined in Chapter 1, depression and burnout are likely to exhibit many similar symptoms; however, depression has a much lower likelihood of going away when factors related to the stressors are dealt with. Recovering from depression often requires the help of a qualified professional.

Irritability

Irritability may take the form of having a short temper or being short of patience when dealing with people or situations perceived to be causes of stress. Individuals may also feel frustration or even anger when faced with situations perceived to be further using up their resources.

Cognitive Impairment

Exhaustion, irritability, cynicism, and other similar symptoms may lead to cognitive impairment, where the individual is unable to focus on their task or make sound decisions. Mistakes and procrastination (to avoid more mistakes) may be associated with cognitive impairment.

Chapter 2 in 100ish words

- Burnout can be caused by factors at the individual, organisational, interrelationship, and societal levels.
- Workers are most likely to experience burnout in occupations where there is frequent exposure to other people and exposure to traumatic content. However, any occupation and sector have the potential to cause people to experience burnout.
- There's a higher likelihood that people with a "Type A" personality will experience burnout, rather than any demographic factors.
- The most prominent sign of burnout is changes in an individual's usual behaviour patterns.
- Symptoms of burnout include mental and physical exhaustion, cynicism, anxiety, depression, irritability, and cognitive impairment.

Chapter 3:
This is how you prevent burnout

In Chapter 2, we broadly discussed what can cause burnout and what symptoms can arise from people experiencing burnout. As you can imagine, the path to preventing burnout involves identifying these causes of stress and reducing them if they are currently present or mitigating the risk of these stressors becoming an issue in the future. It is impossible to completely prevent all risks, but it is a goal for an organisation to minimise as many risks as possible and for the individual to minimise their susceptibility to stressors. Chapter 4 will provide some strategies for recovering from burnout when symptoms have already occurred in individuals.

Identify the risks

Mitigating the risk of a situation or stimulus becoming a stressor requires identifying the risk and implementing appropriate, relevant, and reasonable prevention strategies to reduce the chances that the stimulus becomes a stressor.

Identify Occupational Risks

As discussed earlier, some risks are very difficult to mitigate in certain occupations, for example, those that, by necessity, involve exposure to a traumatic environment. Again, organisations of this nature will need to have in place systems to minimise exposure to traumatic materials and systems to adaptably react and help affected individuals have access to workplace psychosocial health support. For other occupations where there is not, necessarily, an expectation of exposure to stressful stimuli, this is where the consultation process comes in. Organisations need to identify, through consultation with workers, supervisors, and management they are responsible for, possible causes of stress that are known or likely to arise. Yes, this requires an investment of organisational resources, but when empowered to do so, individuals who have knowledge, skills, and experience in an occupation will be able to identify to organisational leadership what could possibly become a stressor in their occupation. Of course, not every possible environmental stressor can be reasonably addressed, but for an organisation, consultation with frontline workers will help leadership prioritise risks.

If you are an individual without the support of an organisation, you may need to undertake this occupational risk consultation process with yourself or a trusted friend or advisor. Write down a list of what you perceive could be stressors in your work or life responsibilities and then prioritise the risks by ranking them from '1' being the most likely cause of stress through to the final stressor. It may help to share your list with your trusted friend or advisor and see if they can identify anything you missed in your responsibilities. Of course, once you have your list, the next step should be to think through which prevention strategies may help mitigate each unique stressor. Reading through Part 2 of this book may help give you ideas.

Identify Organisational Risks

For the individual, the organisation in which they are involved presents potential environmental risks that may cause them to experience stress and burnout. If you are a leader in an organisation, identifying these risks of stressors may not necessarily be a fun process. Given the interpersonal perspectives on burnout, leaders need to be prepared that they may not agree with the risks presented by workers, as workers may perceive risks to the behaviours of other people, including leadership. It is important to remember that in a risk consultation process, the perceived risks and stressors workers present may be just that; perceptions. But for a leader to get defensive or dismissive of perceived risks is to invalidate the workers, which can be a stressful situation and a path to burnout for the worker in itself!

To identify organisational risks, organisations can consult with organisational consultants or other management knowledge workers in the same sector. However, many organisational risks will be unique to each organisation and most easily identified by those who would be affected by the stressors, which are, the organisation's stakeholders.

Identify Individual Risks

As discussed in Chapter 2, several personal attributes are more likely to be associated with a person experiencing burnout. One can take many of the numerous psychometric tests out there to identify if an individual is more prone to "Type A" personality traits, but this is prone to issues of labelling and even preoccupations with over-simplified personality 'types', which are not necessarily fixed over time or circumstances.

If you are an organisation attempting to identify individuals at a higher risk of burnout, this can lead to many false positives because those who have the attributes of a "Type A" personality, including being ambitious and competitive, are probably going to be the best-performing workers if an environment is created for them to thrive without getting caught up in their own drives. Instead, an organisation's best approach is to identify, again through consultation with each individual, their values and priorities, and how those values and priorities align/misalign with the organisation. This is a difficult type of consultation, especially in situations when there is mistrust between stakeholders because you are asking the individual to be completely vulnerable.

If you are an individual attempting to identify if you are at a higher risk of burnout, the best way to do this is to identify what your values are in life; what drives you forward every day. Then, identify which of these values are aligned with or connected with specific work or life responsibilities. For example, Jonathon has the value of 'high achievement' associated with high university work. To identify how this personal value may cause stress in the activity, you could imagine that the phone is about to ring and someone will tell you that you are no longer allowed to do that activity, leaving those values unmet. Did your heart skip a beat, or your blood pressure rose a little when you imagined that value being unmet through having a barrier to the activity that would enable it to be met? If so, then those activities are the ones in which there may be an increased risk of you experiencing burnout when barriers prevent you from completing them in the way that you believe they need to be completed.

What organisational strategies help prevent burnout?

While Part 2 covers prevention strategies in the context of specific stressors, this section addresses some top-level prevention strategies that can help mitigate systematic issues of stress among an organisation's stakeholders. While the organisation will never be able to prevent 100% of risks, it is still its responsibility to take reasonable steps to minimise foreseeable psychological risks.

Manage Expectations

Communication between the individual and the organisation should not only be filled with 'values' and 'mission statements', etc., that are open to interpretation. Individuals can experience stress from a misallocation of their resources and focus due to miscommunication or misinterpretation of the organisation's goals or expectations of the individual's outputs. The organisation needs to manage the individual's expectations through reasonably transparent communications.

This is one type of risk that can be largely mitigated early in an individual's tenure with the organisation, even before they begin working at your organisation. We are talking here about managing expectations when presenting a candidate with their proposed job outline. If a candidate is told they will be doing X, but after being in the job for weeks or months, they are instead doing Y or, even more likely, X plus Y, this is a case of mismanaged expectation. This could have been an oversight or miscommunication during the recruitment process, hopefully unintentional. Misalignment of expectations is very hard to recover from. The individual either works extra hard or has extra pressure put upon them to meet their supervisor's expectations, increasing their mental and physical exhaustion. During the recruitment process, the organisation is the expert on the work and expectations required in the organisation, even if the candidate is an expert in their field. The organisation is also likely to be the expert again on organisational system stressors. It is much better to align the candidate's expectations of the probable potential stressors (e.g., "You will be dealing with other group members for your assignment who will likely have different grade goals than you") than have this misalignment of expectations come up later and lead to the individual experiencing related burnout.

As organisational goals shift over time and individuals are needed to do Y instead of X, or X and Y, this is still where managing expectation comes in. If the organisation requires the individual to do Y instead of X, has the individual been given a reasonable warning and means to request support and resources (e.g., training) to make the transition? If the organisation requires the individual to do X and Y, again, has the individual been given a reasonable warning and means to request support, resources, or consultation on the limits of their resources in completing X and Y? Finally, if the organisation has mismanaged expectations, the most important thing for leadership to do is acknowledge the mismanagement and listen and act appropriately in response to the concerns of the individuals who are affected.

Communicate organisational values

Related to managing expectations is the communication of organisational values. They need to be communicated as clearly as possible to relevant stakeholders so that they know exactly where to focus their limited resources of time, mental and physical energy, and focus. It can be a frequent stressor when the individual believes that an organisation's value is A (e.g., achieving high levels of customer satisfaction), and so the individual devotes so much energy to achieving A, only to find that the organisational leaders are actually looking for B (e.g., achieve increased customer spend). This can create friction in relationships between leaders and other stakeholders when the organisation does not communicate values.

To really drive this point home, communicating an organisational mission statement or even having a list of "values" more suitable for client marketing efforts plopped on pretty posters around the office is not going to help stakeholders understand the organisation. This is about, in the frankest way possible, communicating the organisation's highest priorities to the stakeholders responsible for achieving those priorities. For most commercial organisations, this is likely going to be something related to returns and growth. In practice, to get down to a very specific application, the shareholders in a business might not care whether the sales manager can optimise the appearance of a graph in a report if it does not increase the overall chance of clients paying more, or more clients contracting with the organisation. For Jonathon, his university's priority may not be that he gets along with his group members but rather that they produce a report that does an excellent job meeting the marking criteria.

As we will discuss in the next section, What individual strategies help prevent burnout?, the organisation needs to make sure that relevant outcome-responsible individuals not only understand the organisational values but also that the outcome-responsible individuals align with the organisational values.

Enforce realistic workloads

It is not helpful to the individual for the organisation to turn a blind eye to the individual's workload and allow them to self-manage it. Many individuals will under or overwork based on the organisation's expectations when the organisation's work expectations are not clearly communicated. The goals of supportive management and healthy workplace cultures suggest that stakeholder supervision includes enforcing realistic workload expectations.

To reiterate, the individual should not be the one guessing what their workload should be. Jonathon should not need to guess how many words his assignment should be. This is a ripe recipe for overworking to meet unknown expectations. Instead, supervisors should, if required after consultation with the individual, decide what is a realistic workload for each individual considering their tasks, roles, responsibilities, and sometimes even differing resource limits. There may even be situations when an individual needs to be reprimanded if they continually overwork beyond the reasonable, set expectations of workloads. This is because it can potentially exacerbate a culture of overworking and use up that individual's resource limits, leading to their burnout.

Allow for clearly defined autonomy

I'm sure you have heard that people need autonomy; that is, they need to be able to make choices about what they do and how they do it. But here is a conundrum: How can a supervisor and a worker simultaneously have autonomy? The supervisor autonomously decides that X should be done in a certain way, while the worker believes that X should be done differently. If the supervisor gets their way, the worker's autonomy is reduced and vice versa. The answer to this conundrum is where values and goals need to be openly communicated, and roles, tasks and responsibilities need to be clearly defined.

When there is a lack of clarity, the first conversation between a worker and supervisor shouldn't start with "How do we do X?"; instead, it should be "Who is responsible for X?". Once this is defined, then the collaborative process may begin. By clearly defining and setting the expectations for who is responsible for X, then a consultative process can begin where each party can work within their clearly defined autonomy.

Consult with stakeholders

The expert on what resources are required to complete a given worker's task is nine times out of 10, beyond training, the worker. The individual responsible for the task is the one who will best understand the requirements of their tasks and the most efficient and effective ways of achieving their tasks. If they're not, it is likely because of a miscommunication or the individual's misinterpretation of the organisation's goals and values. The worker is going to be the one who can identify the barriers that prevent them from getting their work done. If they struggle to identify the barriers, then it is possible that they themselves are creating barriers due to their own personal values (e.g., perfectionism), or it is because there are not clearly defined organisational values for the individual to try to achieve.

This is all to say that a very important part of preventing burnout in individuals is for an organisation to have a healthy feedback culture. This is not just having a suggestion box. It is about creating a culture where individuals can openly communicate perceived issues and stressors. Naturally, the individual will have some trepidation about giving certain types of feedback. A barrier to feedback may be fear of being fired or retribution when they feel they need to criticise a manager. Another barrier could be self-doubt over whether an issue is, in fact, an external or internal stressor. These apprehensions can be neatly summed up into the idea that people are often resistant to giving feedback because they are concerned that their feedback will not be heard for what it is. Overcoming this requires a work culture where all stakeholders in the organisation, from workers to supervisors to leadership, learn how to give constructive criticism and receive criticism. Easier said than done, I know. No one likes to be criticised.

One solution for transforming the consultation process from a process that induces fear for all, both the givers and takers, into one that creates safety for feedback exchange is to clearly define and communicate the organisation's values and clearly define individuals' tasks, roles, and responsibilities. That way, feedback that comes through consultations can always be brought back to how barriers and stressors are related to misalignments, miscommunications or misinterpretations of those clearly defined values, goals, and responsibilities.

Jonathon might complain, "My course coordinator has no idea what he's talking about, making me work with these other students who could not care less." If this feedback made its way back to the course coordinator, they might be able to recognise that there was a misunderstanding that the group project wasn't just about producing the report but also looking at the ability of the students to work with others, as reflected in the marking rubric.

A burnout prevention checklist for organisations

Here is a practical list that can be used to assess the extent to which your organisation is preventing burnout. This list focuses more on top-level, general preventative measures that will reduce the chance of stressors occurring within the organisation. Please note this checklist is not a 'one and done' approach. Research suggests that burnout prevention needs to be an ongoing solution, which makes sense given the constantly shifting nature of organisations and the stakeholders involved.

Area	Preventative Action	Further Consideration
Systems	Simplify systems	Are system usage requirements reduced only to what is crucially relevant for stakeholders? Are systems easy to use?
	Increase system support	Are crucial systems well documented? Is system support easily accessible?
Tasks	Clearly define tasks	Do all stakeholders know exactly what is required for every task, eliminating any guesswork?
	Plan task management	Are adequate resources available for the completion of tasks? Is time management of tasks being planned through consultation with the person performing the task?
	Increase task autonomy	Are stakeholders empowered and protected to complete their clearly defined tasks and roles in the way they see fit?

Area	Preventative Action	Further Consideration
Relationships	Clearly define roles	Do all stakeholders know exactly who is responsible for every task/ goal?
	Provide conflict management support	Are there accessible mechanisms for appropriately dealing with conflicts? Are conflict management solutions well promoted and encouraged before things escalate?
Individuals	Provide accessible support	Are there accessible mechanisms for individuals to receive counselling or training?
	Provide feedback	Are there reward incentives for encouraging individuals? Are there constructive feedback mechanisms available for stakeholders throughout their tenure?
	Consult on values	Have the values of each individual been explored to determine how they align or conflict with the organisation?

What individual strategies help prevent burnout?

In the previous section, we covered top-level strategies an organisation could implement to help prevent stressors for individuals. However, it must be stated that there are limits to what organisations can do to prevent individuals from experiencing burnout. Factors of burnout prevention also need to be addressed by the individuals themselves.

Identify your values and goals to be ready for barriers

As discussed in Chapter 2, the factors that allow environmental stressors to affect individuals are likely to vary from person to person, and a stressor will affect everyone differently. Some stressors are processed consciously, also known as 'top-down', where a stimulus is perceived as stressful due to how the individual perceives it. Others are processed subconsciously, also known as 'bottom-up', where the stressor affects us, but we aren't necessarily able to pinpoint why. An initial strategy for preventing burnout is for individuals to identify environmental stressors and barriers and consider how they may consciously process these to affect us. This requires deep personal introspection, and we need to be able to identify our own personal values and goals. Pragmatically, one method is to write down your personal values and goals relating to your work. Then, identify which tasks, people, or situations may act as barriers to your values or goals. These barriers are likely to cause stress.

Speaking personally, I have had to identify that my own need for perfectionism likely comes from my desire to impress certain people by "proving them wrong", showing that I can succeed in certain areas where they said I would fail. Overcoming this stressor required me to identify why I was seeking the approval of these people. After introspecting about what values and goals are important to me in life, I grew apathetic about whether these people saw me succeed or fail.

Jonathan may need to consider that working with others may be a recurring stressor, as he views others as barriers to his success rather than as collaborators or contributors. Another example: an individual may identify that the organisation they are involved with requires quick project turnaround times. If the individual knows they have perfectionist tendencies due to their value of high-quality work, they may identify that these turnaround times could become a future stressor.

Identify the source of stressors and barriers and take steps to prevent

How do we prevent the potential barriers identified above from becoming real stress and a potential cause of burnout? A good starting point is to identify the extent to which the stressor is related to your values or the environment. Take the scenario above regarding fast project turnaround times: are they perceived as quick because the individual does not think the projects can be completed to their perception of high-quality work in the given time, or is it perceived as quick because the individual does not think that the projects can be done in time to meet the client's high-quality expectations? In other words, individuals need to identify whether preventing stressors requires them to change anything about their own perceptions of the situation or whether there is an external cause.

If the individual determines that the stressor is due to their own perceptions of high-quality work, then the prevention strategy is to identify what drives these perceptions and whether these perceptions can be adapted, given their clearly defined roles, tasks, and responsibilities with their limited available resources. Additionally, if the barrier is internal, the individual needs to identify whether there may be a more appropriate place to meet these needs. For example, if high-quality work is a goal, the individual might pursue an alternative hobby (e.g., art) outside of work where the goal is high-quality work. This allows the fast turnaround projects to meet another of the individual's values or goals, such as skill development around project management or financial goals.

If an individual identifies that a stressor or barrier is external, then there may be systematic organisational issues, such as insufficient time for each project. This would require the individual to approach organisational decision-makers to suggest changes. This can be intimidating for the individual. They may feel that they are inevitably criticising one of the decision-makers, admitting to their own incompetence, and worry that they may be punished by decision-makers, even if the issue is systematic. It is unfortunate to say that these are indeed real possibilities. One would be dishonest to suggest otherwise. This, of course, is why many organisational systematic issues never actually get resolved. Refer to "What organisational strategies help prevent burnout?" for suggestions on how feedback can best be approached by referencing clearly defined roles, tasks, and responsibilities. For example, when addressing the issue of projects requiring turnaround times that you believe are too quick, the discussion should centre on how the process of completing the project differs from the clearly defined expectations of the project. If expectations are clearly defined and managed for all stakeholders (including clients), it allows issues to be discussed in terms of the expectations of the organisation's outputs, not the performance of any individuals.

To summarise this section, the best approach for an individual to prevent stressors and burnout is to identify potential causes and develop steps to mitigate these stressors. Mitigating stressors requires identifying not only the potential causes, but also the true sources of these causes.

A burnout prevention checklist for individuals

This is truly a top-level, non-stressor-specific checklist of actions an individual can undertake to put peripheral preventative measures in place so that these areas in the checklist do not become distractions or exacerbations when specific stressors enter their lives. As with the burnout prevention checklist for organisations, this is not a 'one and done' approach but rather the beginning of a lifelong journey of being mindful of what actions can help or hinder stressors and burnout.

Area	Preventative Action	Further Consideration
Physical	Increase physical activity	Are there any activities (e.g., listening to podcasts/audiobooks, talking to others) that could be done while conducting physical activity? Are there any sedentary activities that could be switched out for a physical one?
	Get adequate sleep	Are the activities you are doing right before bed (e.g., going on your phone/computer, drinking coffee) hindering your sleep patterns?
	Increase healthy eating	Are there certain eating habits that could be combatted through mindful eating? (That is, thinking about what, when, and why you are eating).

Area	Preventative Action	Further Consideration
Emotional	Increase social support	Do you have others to whom you can turn for accountability and support in making good choices?
	Increase social activities	Are there hobbies/groups you could join that would enable you to participate in self-building social activities?
	Increase emotional knowledge	Are you aware of the emotions you are experiencing throughout the day?
Resources	Ensure adequate resources	Do you have the adequate resources (that is, time and ability) to complete your required tasks?
	Prepare resource support	Do you have a plan for obtaining extra resources/help for when you do not have adequate resources?
Values	Seek value alignment	Does the organisation align with your personal values? Is there someone in the organisation with whom you can have a frank, safe conversation regarding this?

Chapter 3 in 100ish words

- Organisations can prevent burnout by identifying risks through consultation, managing stakeholder expectations, communicating organisational values, enforcing realistic workloads, and facilitating clearly defined autonomy.
- Burnout can be prevented in individuals by identifying their own values and goals and identifying 1) how these are or are not met through their work, 2) what barriers may prevent them from achieving these values or goals, and how these can be mitigated.
- Many practical steps can be taken to prevent burnout from being experienced in both the organisation and the individual, but there are no 'one and done' approaches.

Chapter 4:
This is how you remedy burnout

Burnout prevention is great, but it's obviously not much help when you're already in the thick of it. This chapter suggests solutions for when individuals are already experiencing stressors and burnout. As a reminder, burnout describes negative symptoms resulting from stressful stimuli.

There may be opportunities for these types of strategies to be implemented on a large scale (e.g., in group settings). Still, it is more likely that the strategies will be undertaken by individuals. It is also true and relevant that some strategies will work very well for some people but be ineffective for others. You can think of the solutions and strategies in this chapter as a "menu" of possible solutions to help. In the best-case scenario, someone experiencing burnout will work with a professional to determine the best and most relevant solutions, but in the absence of that, if an individual can work on clearly identifying the exact sources and causes of their stressors and symptoms, they will be able to better determine the most relevant interventions.

What strategies help for short-term coping with burnout symptoms?

Short-term coping strategies aim to enable the individual to keep functioning despite there not being an immediate solution to the causes of stressors and burnout they are experiencing. Here, we may divide the strategies into those focused on the physical and the mental; however, there is much crossover.

Physical Strategies

When you are facing stressors, it is important not to add any further stressors to your body by making unhealthy decisions around your physical behaviours. Examples of unhelpful choices may be staying up late binge-watching television to escape your thoughts, rather than sleeping; snacking all day on high-sugar foods to experience moments of pleasure when you're feeling down; not doing any physical movement during the day.

Your physical reaction to stressors might be the complete opposite, and you can't do anything but sleep; you may not feel like eating anything at all; you might go to the gym and exercise excessively to chase a high. First, these are all natural responses to stressors, and again, your physical behaviour decisions in reaction to stress are likely going to be very different to those of your co-worker next to you who is also facing burnout and stress, probably grounded in what you know gave you relief the last time you felt a stressful situation.

To start, here are two basic, good physical health choices:

1. Get an adequate amount of sleep every night. Not too much, and not too little. Each individual's Goldilocks level of sleep tends to be different, so this may require keeping track of your sleep and wake times, as well as what activities you perform before bed and how you feel when you first wake up and an hour or two after you wake up. With this information, you can start to gauge what your personal amount of optimal sleep is.

There are also sleep issues for many people dealing with burnout, such as insomnia, inability to sleep quickly, or waking up during the night with thoughts that won't go away. This is where the cognitive meets the physical. Look at the exercises coming up for cognitive defusion and mindfulness techniques that aim to help you pause thinking on a given thought for enough time to allow yourself to rest and process the thoughts at a more appropriate time (a.k.a., not when you're trying to sleep). Practically, if you are in bed and cannot fall asleep within a short period of time, you are better off leaving the bed and doing a non-stimulating activity (e.g., reading a book, not using your phone, TV, or gaming) until you feel sleepy enough to try again.

2. Eat mindfully. Here, being mindful of what you eat simply means thinking about what you are doing to enable you to make more informed decisions about your choices. This is rather than suggesting a specific diet that cuts X out but adds in Y, but only for 8.6 hours a day, 3.7 days per week. Yes, there are inevitably foods that, if you overconsume, you will be more likely to feel tired and lethargic due to highs and crashes. The strategy in mindful eating is, before you consume any food, beverage, or drugs, ask yourself the questions, "Why

am I wanting to consume this? What emotion am I currently feeling? What has happened in the last hour? What outcome am I seeking from consuming this?".

To illustrate, I'm sitting here writing this book at 10:15 in the morning on a Wednesday. I know that there is a large box of chocolates in the kitchen pantry, from which I am considering choosing a treat. Why do I want to consume a chocolate? Because I crave the taste of sugar; because writing this section is slightly less exciting than writing some of the other sections and the chocolate might give me a bit of a high. What emotion am I currently feeling? I'm feeling content but also unfocused and pressured to finish this book. What happened in the last hour? In the last hour, I have been sitting here at my computer, focusing quite hard on my writing. What outcome am I seeking from consuming a chocolate? I want to feel good; I want to feel enjoyment; I want a momentary distraction from my writing.

After I've answered all these questions, I have concluded that it is not specifically the chocolate I'm seeking, but rather a break from my writing; to switch to something that might be more enjoyable before returning. A chocolate specifically might actually be less of a relief than taking a slightly longer break.

Cognitive Strategies

Here, we discuss strategies for cognitively coping with burnout, which involve providing methods to help manage your thoughts. As previously mentioned, mental exhaustion is one of the most common symptoms of burnout. This exhaustion often occurs when we haven't given ourselves a break from the constant processing of thoughts. Without rest, we can feel trapped in negative feelings and emotions.

In this section, we explore short-term coping solutions rather than processing strategies for these thoughts (which we will discuss in the next section on long-term solutions to burnout). The goal is to offer some methods that allow you to take a break and gain control over your thoughts by deciding when and where to process stressors. Most of the day is filled with tasks such as work, interactions with family, or sleep, which aren't ideal times for processing stressors and developing action plans to address them.

Identify that your thoughts are just thoughts

It may sound invalidating to simply call your thoughts just thoughts, and some thoughts are concerns very much related to physical outcomes. However, these aren't necessarily the thoughts that we are discussing here. Here, we are talking about unwanted or intrusive thoughts that you suspect do not relate to an immediate stressor that can't be dealt with later. But how do you consciously choose to stop thinking about a given stressor? Stop thinking about pink elephants. Stop thinking about pink elephants. Stop thinking about pink elephants. Being told to stop thinking about something often means you're more likely to just keep thinking about that thing. The most common strategy discussed in psychology for overcoming thoughts is not to try and ignore them or run away from them but rather acknowledge that they are thoughts and deal with them as they are: thoughts.

This brings us into an area of exercises that fall under something called cognitive defusion techniques. In simple terms, these techniques aim to learn that you can distance yourself from your thoughts so that you can re-approach them at a more convenient or appropriate time. For example, one cognitive defusion technique is to simply thank your mind. To illustrate: When my mind is concerned about whether I made a mistake on the report that we just sent to the client, I can say, 'Thank you, mind, for bringing this to my attention'. Just because my mind was concerned that there might have been a mistake on the report does not necessarily mean that there was, in fact, a mistake on the report. My mind made a thought. It did not create a reality. So, I can say "thank you" and move on with my day until I can consider whether adding any error-checking mechanisms to my workflow would be beneficial.

Another technique is to give the thought a name. From the example I discussed above, I might name that thought my "I wonder if I made a mistake?" thought. And yes, that is a regular thought that I have. However, the "I wonder if I made a mistake?" thought is just a thought. Again, thinking it has not made a mistake appear. Naming the thought makes the thought more abstract as an entity, rather than a reality.

Other techniques can be used to turn the thought into a meaningless reduction. Say the word over and over: 'mistake, mistake, mistake, mistake'... until you hear it's just a series of sounds. Some have said that singing the thought can turn a threat into a humorous notion:

(To the tune of Twinkle Twinkle Little Star)
I wonder if I made a mistake?
Mistake, mistake, mistake, mistake.

Another broad set of techniques involves the visualisation of thoughts. One can use many different visual metaphors to distance thoughts from oneself. One technique is to try visualising the thought as a physical object. That is, try to visualise the thought as having a colour, shape, texture, and size. Here, you are turning the thought into something tangible rather than an intrusive, recurring abstract thought you're unsure what to do with. Another technique involves visualising the thought as a specific object which you can observe from afar. For example, you may have heard of the visualisation of thinking about thoughts as cars passing by in traffic. You can sit on the side of the road and see the thoughts crossing in front of you, possibly even driving back and forth and honking for your attention. You can just continue sitting by the side of the road and watch the thoughts go by, without interacting with them. A similar idea is seeing the thoughts as leaves floating down the river. They can just float by. You don't need to jump into the river to pick up the leaves and look at them closely. Another example is seeing the thoughts as clouds floating through the sky far off in the distance. You can choose to watch the clouds, or you can choose to look at something closer by, like the grass at your feet or the book in your hand.

Mindfulness

Probably the most discussed technique for combating symptoms of stress and burnout is mindfulness. Much has been written about mindfulness and meditation—so much so that it can become quite confusing as to what exactly we're meant to do when practising 'mindfulness'. Mindfulness doesn't need to involve any advanced or specific ideologies, philosophies, or religious beliefs. Practising mindfulness simply means focusing on being present in the moment. The goal is to learn how to choose what you think about and where you want your attention to be.

Let me give you a very simple mindfulness exercise you can do to illustrate:

1. Find a quiet place where you won't be disturbed. Put your phone on silent. Turn off your computer screen.

2. Sit or lie in a comfortable position. We're not looking for any fancy yoga poses here.

3. Close your eyes.

4. Think about your breathing. Think about the air entering through your mouth or nose, filling up your lungs, and then leaving your body again. Continue to do this for a minute or so.

5. If you find your mind wandering away from focusing on your breathing, try to bring your focus back onto your breathing. Acknowledge the thought or feeling for what it is, but then return to focusing on your breathing.

6. After focusing just on your breathing for a few minutes (if you're focusing on a specific amount of time, you're not focusing on your breathing), try focusing on the environment around you. This may be the sound of birds or traffic in the distance. It might be the temperature of the room. It may be how the chair or floor feels on your skin.

7. After focusing on your environment for a few minutes, focus on your breathing again.

8. After focusing on your breathing for a few minutes, try focusing on every part of your body, starting from your feet all the way up to the top of your head. Starting with your feet: How do they feel? What are they pressing against? What temperature do they feel?

9. Shift your focus to your ankles for a moment, then your calves, knees, thighs, hips, stomach, chest, back, hands, arms, shoulders, face, and head.

10. After focusing on each part of your body, bring your focus back to the time and place in which you are sitting or lying.

If you have done the exercise, you will by now realize that you are choosing where you are focusing your attention. You are focusing on your breathing, then your environment, then your body. There is a high chance that as soon as you focus back on the time and place in which you are sitting or lying, thoughts about the events in the past or situations to be addressed in the future will come flooding back. But now, if you have completed the exercise, you have evidence that you can choose where your attention is. If you do not want your attention to be on a stressor at that time, you can focus on something else. This will give you a moment to rest or have resilience during a stressful event.

Additionally, practising being present in the moment has other benefits. Focusing your attention on the immediate environment can help you improve your concentration on a given task. It can also help you better engage with those around you because if you are present with the person, you will be able to be more attentive to their emotions and what they are trying to communicate. Finally, mindfulness may also help you to identify behaviours, thoughts, or feelings that are more of a hindrance than a help. After identification, these may be targeted for change or improvement.

Some of you may have balked at the mindfulness exercise I outlined above, which is fine: it's not everybody's cup of tea, and mileage may vary as to its effectiveness. But even without the exercise, the principle of mindfulness holds: Negative thoughts can be held in check and emotional exhaustion minimised by learning to focus on the present moment.

What strategies help with long-term fixing burnout?

The short-term coping strategies outlined above are good for a quick fix, but when a really real, specific burnout stressor is present, they are just that: a quick fix. They are not addressing the core causes of stress and burnout. Here, we are looking at strategies to try and overcome burnout in the long term. In many ways, these strategies are the application of burnout prevention, which means a long-term remedy will look different depending on the stressor. Again, you need to consider the cause of the stressor and burnout to know the relevant solution or strategy.

The stark reality of any stressor is that there will eventually be an endpoint. In some situations, the endpoint can be brought about by your own actions, such as leaving a job or switching projects, but in numerous situations, the endpoint is outside of your control. The one thing you do have control over, and therefore can create an endpoint for, is the extent to which you have the knowledge and expertise to deal with the stressor cognitively and emotionally. Here we are addressing three common cognitive symptoms of burnout: cynicism, a sense of ineffectiveness, and cognitive deficits. These have the potential to be long-lasting symptoms after experiencing burnout and, if left unaddressed, have the potential to negatively affect future endeavours.

Overcoming cynicism

Cynicism is where you have certain sceptical beliefs about the situation around you. In the context of burnout, cynicism is usually along the lines of being cynical that things will ever improve, that people around you will ever change for the better, or that the demands on your resources will ever slow down. This can cause you to have a pessimistic outlook on your life.

The first strategy for overcoming cynicism is to challenge your beliefs. This is to understand if your beliefs are grounded in the evidence of the objective environmental stressors. A question may be: What evidence do you have that situation will not soon change? There may be repeated, chronic evidence of a given situation being stressful, so this would be a time when the stressor needs to be reduced or mitigated. Another situation could be a nagging client with very specific project requirements. What evidence is there that they will continue to be nagging on other aspects or that they will not change if you take a different approach to project communications? What about the supervisor who you are cynical about, whether they care for anything else in the world except for themselves? But do you have evidence for that? Have you approached them with your specific needs and concerns? Unfortunately, a lot of cynicism can simply come from observing repeating patterns. Why would the stressor you have experienced time and time again ever stop?

When there is clear evidence that your cynicism is founded, but you still would like to reduce your cynicism in the face of non-changing stressors, that requires strategies that will help you gain new perspectives on your situation. Please note, I don't suggest any of these strategies flippantly, but you may need to pick and try to find strategies that work for you. One perspective shift strategy can be trying to see if there are any positive aspects of the situation. Is there anything you can be grateful for that you feel could come out of the stressor you're experiencing? Examples could be how much you have learned about how personally you react to stressors that could be applied to avoiding future, similar stressors.

Another perspective shift could be considering the stressor from another person's perspective. If your supervisor is driving you up the wall with request after request, try considering what emotions, motivations, or feelings your supervisor may be experiencing that drive their relentless requests. It's possible they are feeling pressure from their supervisor. This could help you identify that many situations are highly complex and there are, very rarely, people who are "pure evil" and out to get you. Everybody has their own motivations (for example, fear or success) for doing things that affect other people. Here, you are attempting to develop empathy for the experiences of people around you and gain an understanding of why they are afflicting a stressor onto you. This is not in pursuit of justifying bad behaviour but gaining insight into their drivers.

It can often be very difficult to get a new perspective for yourself, and that is where it can be great to actually get the perspective of positive influences around you. Find a trusted friend, colleague, or mentor and express to them what your cynical thoughts are. What are you cynical about that you think will never change or about others' motivations? They might just be able to see something about you or your situation that you cannot. They may also be able to give you an outsider's perspective into the extent to which your stressor will repeat in the future or whether the stressors were a unique combination of factors for which you do not need to be as cynical about in the future.

Overcoming a sense of ineffectiveness

Ineffectiveness is when you feel like your efforts are worthless or the work you are doing ultimately has no meaning. For obvious reasons, this can be debilitating and be highly associated with feeling emotionally exhausted as you try to find meaning in what you do, which can also be associated with feelings of guilt and shame. Additionally, especially given we often have a unique mix of roles, tasks, and responsibilities to which we have no one to compare against, we can be quite poor at judging our own performance and effectiveness.

Much like cynicism, overcoming a sense of ineffectiveness needs to start with challenging your beliefs in this area. What evidence is there that your work is ineffective? Is your work effective in helping a specific person, even if that person is not someone you necessarily like? Is your work effective even to the basic point of simply allowing you to have an income for your personal livelihood? A good starting point here is to observe what you have achieved. Celebrate those achievements, no matter how small they are! If you can't find anything to celebrate, try asking for the perspective of those around you.

If you perceive that your mistakes outweigh your achievements, or you feel your ineffectiveness is because of your mistakes, it is important to firstly have self-compassion. Nobody on this earth is devoid of mistakes. Yes, some mistakes are big, and some mistakes are small, but self-criticism over mistakes is not ultimately what prevents you from making mistakes in the future. That comes when you learn from your mistakes and learn how to prevent those mistakes from reoccurring in the future. Again, talk to a trusted friend or advisor about the extent to which mistakes were solely driven by individual factors over organisational factors. Talking to them may also help you see a way to remedy mistakes and identify error correction mechanisms that could be implemented to reduce the likelihood of mistakes in the future.

Overcoming cognitive deficits

One factor often associated with burnout is a decline in cognitive functioning, or, in simpler terms, making more mistakes because you're burned out. Given this is one of the more novel researched symptoms of burnout, there are fewer known interventions that can help with this in the long term, but here I offer some simple strategies that follow on from the short-term strategies.

Firstly, learn to focus on your immediate activities and tasks that need attention. Learn to focus on being in the present to concentrate on identifying the essential needs of tasks and what error-checking mechanisms you might need to put in place. Make good physical health choices, including personally relevant limits on consumption of anything that may cause you to not be able to focus on your tasks, and pursue habits that contribute to a clear, focused mind (e.g., exercise and sleep routines).

Poor choices can lead to poor choices in a cycle, which is why cognitive deficits can be a long-term problem that requires making choices that will break a cycle. Breaking a cycle of bad habits can be difficult due to misinformed approaches or a lack of motivation. It is recommended to talk to an experienced mental health professional if you feel that there is a bad habit you cannot break.

Chapter 4 in 100ish words

- Short-term strategies for coping with burnout include making good physical health choices. Cognitive strategies encompass undertaking exercises that identify thoughts as simply being thoughts and learning, through mindfulness, how to choose where you focus your attention and thoughts.

- Long-term strategies for overcoming burnout encompass overcoming cynicism by challenging beliefs and learning how to shift perspectives; overcoming a sense of ineffectiveness by celebrating achievements and working through mistakes, often with the help of others; overcoming cognitive deficits by learning how to focus on your immediate tasks that need attention, making good choices, and seeking help when unable to break out of cycles of bad choices.

Chapter 5:
How To Help Others Who Are Experiencing Burnout

Why should organisations care about burnout?

Let's start off with a discussion for organisational leaders about why they should care about burnout. For this, one could argue several ways to appeal to whatever leaders most value in their organisation. Still, ultimately, an organisation needs to be willing to admit some responsibility for the care of its employees for any discussion of burnout to result in preventative actions.

Various government and non-government organisations recognise the need for organisations to create a safe psychosocial workplace. For example, there is ISO 45003:2021 that provides guidelines for managing psychosocial risks and considers the risks in this area to be largely on par with physical risks. In Australia, there are work, health, and safety laws that state organisations must eliminate or minimise psychosocial risks as far as is reasonably possible [4]. The

UN's International Labour Organization also emphasises the need to minimise exposure to psychosocial hazards to avoid the outcomes of stress and burnout [5].

The exact legislation on the responsibility of the organisation in this area will vary between legal frameworks, so it is highly recommended that organisational leadership stakeholders seek clarity on the legal requirements and responsibilities of the organisation in this area. Providing actual legal advice is beyond the scope of this book, but the general aim of these laws is to create a framework within which it can be examined whether an individual's psychological injury was a result of or contributed to by employment activities, and to what extent an organisation took reasonable actions to prevent the injury occurrence.

Beyond the legal requirements of creating a safe workplace environment, I believe it is an organisation's ethical or moral obligation to take care of employees. Organisation employees, members and other relevant stakeholders are humans who have worth and dignity and, therefore, should be treated with respect. They have lives outside of the organisation. They have hopes and dreams. In nearly every instance, an individual wants to do their best and contribute to the company's success. For this reason, it is right for the organisation to reciprocate this by contributing to the success of the individual.

How do you talk to people experiencing burnout?

Many of us have been in contact with someone experiencing stress and burnout. At the time, you might not have realised exactly what they were going through, either because they were not communicating the full extent of their experience (it is common for people to downplay their situation by saying things like, "I'm stressed, but fine") or you weren't aware of the signs of burnout. But being around someone who is experiencing burnout can be very difficult, whether you're their spouse, friend, or colleague. Their exhaustion, disengagement, anxieties, and cynicism can be quite concerning to watch and may even be causing you issues through second-hand stress.

There are not any major differences that need to be considered when talking to someone experiencing burnout as opposed to another type of emotional distress, except to consider that the burnout is more likely to be focused on a specific aspect of their lives rather than a generalised distress. This is somewhat helpful in that you can provide an easier distraction (if they request it) and relief than other emotionally distressing experiences, but it is difficult in that there may be very specific nuances to their burnout experience and multifaceted factors core to the individual's views and life motivations in that area of stressors.

Here is a helpful list of actions you can take when talking to someone experiencing burnout:

1. Ask whether they'd like to discuss their stressors or be distracted. Different people deal with stressors in different ways, and where one person processes through talking, another may process by thinking. While talking to someone else can really help bring objective perspectives into a situation, the exact time you are engaging with the person experiencing burnout may not be the right time for them. It is entirely appropriate to ask them if they would like to discuss the perceived issues with you, or whether you can provide a distraction through conversing on a different topic. It can also be good to ask if they'd like to be followed up on to converse at a later date.

2. If they are open to talking, pay attention. If they decide they want to discuss their stressors with you, this is a privilege, and it is your role to actively listen and engage with them. Importantly, do not project your own experiences onto them, as every situation, even if they sound quite similar or have very similar symptoms, is possibly going to have very different factors involved. Interjecting their story with your own can invalidate and close the door to vulnerability. Instead, active listening involves you engaging back with them by showing that you have heard them and validating their feelings and emotions. After you have made sure they are validated, then you can gauge whether it is relevant to share your own experiences.

3. Ask before giving advice. Again, if they decide to discuss their stressors with you, it is important that you assess whether they are looking for a listening ear, in which case, engage in active listening or ask if they are looking for advice before giving it. Giving unsolicited advice, again, can be invalidating.

4. If you are close to someone experiencing burnout and want to help them, I suggest looking back at Chapter 4 and gently encouraging the individual to pursue short-term and long-term strategies for overcoming burnout. A good strategy can be asking them if there's an area that you specifically could advocate and support, such as promoting good physical habits, being a listening board for putting boundaries in place at work or identifying achievements. It can also be good to discuss if they would like to do activities with you that aren't work-related and can provide rest and distraction, for a given time, from their exhausting chronic thinking and processing of stressors.

How do you promote healthy organisational cultures?

If you want to create a healthy culture, one really important thing needs to happen in your organisation: As many stakeholders as possible need to be on board. And this means stakeholders from the client-facing sales workers all the way up to the board or senior leadership. This is because as soon as one level of the organisational hierarchy does not see the importance of creating a healthy workplace culture, they will create demands on others that go against the culture. Yes, this is a utopian workplace. Every person in the organisation has their own motivations that will inevitably conflict with other people's motivations. How can we address this? By having clearly defined and realistic roles, responsibilities, and tasks. Only by having clearly defined and realistic roles, responsibilities and tasks can people's actions, regardless of their level in the hierarchy, be assessed as to whether they are within or outside these well-defined and realistic roles, responsibilities, and tasks.

We could list out the basics of what a healthy workplace looks like, which involves open and honest communication, showing respect to others, encouraging healthy work-life balances etc. But I think these ideals are not worth anyone's time unless a healthy workplace culture is promoted by the example of those in leadership roles. So that, I would say, is the most important factor in promoting a healthy workplace culture. If you are a leader wanting to create a healthy workplace, you need to start showing respect; you need to start having a healthy work-life balance; you need to start establishing clear and realistic expectations not only for yourself but also for your employees.

If you are not a manager or supervisor and trying to promote a healthy workplace culture, you can still lead by example. Jump onto every and all helpful initiatives that the workplace is promoting that align with the culture you want to see continue in the organisation. Encourage others around you to have healthy work-life boundaries by not being a source of extra load beyond their available resources. If you truly believe there are areas where your organisation can improve the culture, why not try having a discussion with leadership, offering solution-driven suggestions about what could be improved? Don't dismiss your leadership's willingness to try new things. I know you are likely cynical that they could change their perspective, but here are some tips for how to approach them:

1. Have a clear objective for what you believe could be improved.

2. Outline the problem objectively in the context of clearly defined roles, tasks, and responsibilities and how the problem inhibits the organisation's goals.

3. Offer solutions right after presenting the problem.

4. Listen to your manager's response respectfully and discuss what could be done to implement the solution.

They will have their subjective perspective on the issue. Depending on your relationship with the manager, their response may range from defensiveness to a lack of understanding of the issue to a lack of empathy. You can acknowledge that their response is outside of your control. But I offer the hope that if the problems are presented in the right context of the organisation's goals with clear solutions, there is an increased chance of change occurring to make the organisation culturally healthier.

How do you provide support for those in your organisation experiencing burnout?

If you suspect there are people for whom you are responsible in your organisation experiencing burnout, there are immediate steps you should start to take to avoid the stressors and burnout spreading to others.

The consultation process involves finding out from as many relevant stakeholders as possible what stressors are present in the organisation. Important things here are to ensure the anonymity of the respondents, given there is a likelihood that the stressors have the potential to be critically received; for example, leadership may be a perceived cause of stress. Consultation would ideally involve data collection being completed by a third party or a widely trusted organisation stakeholder (e.g., a human resources officer who is empowered and trusted to securely handle the data). Secondly, it is very important to transparently communicate the aggregate results of such a consultation back to the stakeholders. This is for many reasons, including the message that it sends to stakeholders that leadership has actually processed the consultation results and that none of the results (especially any that are critical of the leadership) have been censored before processing. Immediately following the presentation of consultation results should be the identification of reasonable actions that leadership stakeholders will take to either mitigate the stress or provide further support for stakeholders affected by those stressors.

After the consultation process, actions and changes in support should start taking place to mitigate and prevent the stressors. This, however, comes with some big caveats: There needs to be careful consideration made before implementing changes because there is a high chance that making changes in themselves can actually exacerbate burnout. This is most obviously a problem when decision-makers' inconsistent actions are found to be a cause of burnout. Creating new schemes or systems may just increase stakeholders' cynicism that the inconsistent actions will never stop. An additional time to be cautious about making changes is when there is a high likelihood that the changes will alter or create confusion around responsibilities, for those already experiencing stressors. In situations where it is identified that those two stressors (frequent changes and unclear responsibilities, roles, or tasks) are present, stopping changes can actually be a valid solution until roles, responsibilities and tasks are more clearly defined and understood by all stakeholders. The changes would then align processes and systems to these clearly defined roles, responsibilities, and tasks. Even if the stressors are not specifically related to those two stressors, it is always a valid solution to ensure all stakeholders understand their clearly defined roles, responsibilities, and tasks. Again, any changes are then communicated in the context of these clearly defined roles, responsibilities, and tasks.

It is recommended that, after a formal consultation has taken place, informal consultation follow-ups also take place, focusing on those most likely to be affected by identified stressors. This could be done through conducting periodic check-in meetings with those affected by the stressor to monitor the outcomes of stress prevention actions. Essentially, it is important to ensure implemented actions and supports do what was intended. This could be because the wrong support was implemented for the stressor or those affected are not utilising the support. Either way, the action and support can be assessed from the follow-up check-in meetings.

Healthy culture burnout checklist

The following is a list of checks that stakeholders in your organisation can use to begin creating a healthy work culture to prevent burnout.

- [ ] Are work tasks clearly defined for each person?
- [ ] Are work tasks of reasonable resource expectations for each person?
- [ ] Are the work expectations and tasks of each person clearly communicated to the given person and all co-workers?
- [ ] Are there open paths for remedying conflicts with the clearly defined tasks and roles?
- [ ] Is leadership leading by example for healthy workplace practices?
- [ ] Are there adequate resources available for individuals in situations where there is an imbalance between resources and demands?
- [ ] Is leadership actively encouraging healthy workplace practices?
- [ ] Are leaders/supervisors trained in detecting what the likely signs are that an individual is experiencing burnout?
- [ ] Are there periodic check-in mechanisms to encourage an ongoing conversation about healthy cultures?
- [ ] Is there a system in place for periodic consultation and action planning to stay on top of current and potential stressors?

Chapter 5 in 100ish words

• Organisations have legal, ethical, and moral obligations to take reasonable actions to prevent psychological injury in stakeholders, including that of stress and burnout.

• You can help someone experiencing burnout by engaging with them by talking with them about the stressors or providing distractions from them.

• Organisations can promote a healthy culture by having leadership stakeholders lead by example. Workers can also lead by example in behaviours and activities and be agents of change.

• Providing support for organisational stakeholders experiencing burnout starts with a consultation and then taking action, when appropriate, that addresses stressors.

Chapter 6:
The Actions Of A Person Who Wants To Stop Burnout

Let's summarise everything we have learned so far. The purpose of this chapter, as much as any other, is to provide you with ideas for action. These are things you can start putting in place for yourself personally and any organisations you are involved with.

What did we learn today about preventing burnout?

There is no single thing that an organisation or person can do to make themselves 100% foolproof and resistant to experiencing stress and burnout. As an individual, the best possible actions you can take to prevent burnout involve identifying what risks around you could possibly lead to stress and coming up with a plan for mitigating that risk. Risk mitigation can look like this:

1.   Ensuring you have adequate support at the ready before your resources are imbalanced with the demands.

2.   Identifying what your personal values are and how they align or conflict with the risks.

3.   Ensuring that all your tasks and roles are clearly defined, resource-realistic and mutually understood between yourself and other stakeholders.

Ultimately, you need to have an ongoing consultation with yourself about your life activities and how they align with your core values. Practically, this may result in your having to put in place strict boundaries for when the situations and risks are greater than you are willing to allow, given your core beliefs.

Individual's burnout prevention task list

☐ I have written a list of all possible stressors that may arise due to the environment in which I live or work.

☐ I have written a list of all possible stressors that may arise due to my own goals and values.

☐ I have written resources, support or actions that could help me reduce the risk of each of the environmental and goal/value driven possible stressors.

☐ I have a complete understanding of my responsibilities, roles and tasks in the organisation or work in which I'm involved.

☐ I have communicated with my supervisor any responsibilities, roles, or tasks that I do not understand or believe are not mutually agreed upon.

☐ I have communicated with my supervisor any responsibilities, roles, or tasks that I do not believe are realistic demands on my available resources.

If you are a managing stakeholder in an organisation, your best path to preventing burnout, as discussed in Chapter 5, is to ensure that all tasks, roles, and responsibilities are clearly defined, realistic for the resources available, understood and communicated to all other stakeholders in the organisation. It's vital that the tasks, roles, and responsibilities are realistic for what each person can reasonably achieve and they are adequately resourced to do so. Again, I also emphasise that the individual may not be the best judge of what they can reasonably achieve, as they are likely to overestimate what they can achieve. Finally, preventing burnout requires creating a healthy workplace culture where leadership stakeholders lead by example in the behaviours and actions they take.

Real talk for organisations: there are times when individuals are not able to take the appropriate steps to remedy burnout that is not, in fact, exacerbated or caused at all by the organisation and is instead driven by the individual's choices, beliefs or a lack of personal resources to meet the reasonable demands of the role, task or responsibilities. If the organisation has taken reasonable actions to minimise the individual's psychosocial risks, especially after they are aware or have identified that an individual might be engaging in any unhelpful behaviours, there do come situations when it is necessary to evaluate not only the extent to which the job performance is affected by the individual's behaviours, beliefs and resource capacity but also the extent to which they are inflicting stressors onto other stakeholders in the organisation. These situations would be when human resource policies need to be enacted.

But, to end this section on a positive note, there are so many actions that can be taken to prevent burnout, and although the actions will differ depending on the stressor, there is still a guiding principle, both for individuals and organisations, that burnout can be prevented by having realistic, well-defined, adequately resourced tasks, roles and responsibilities that are understood by all relevant stakeholders.

Organisation's burnout prevention task list

☐ Each individual's role, tasks and responsibilities are realistic to what the individual can reasonably achieve.

☐ Each individual's role, tasks and responsibilities are clearly defined, in writing.

☐ Each individual's role, tasks and responsibilities are understood by the individual.

☐ Each individual's role, tasks and responsibilities are understood by the other relevant stakeholders.

☐ Each individual is consulted for their resource capacity to meet the reasonable requirements of their role, tasks, and responsibilities.

☐ There is a system in place for individuals to communicate, without judgement, perceived stressors and request relevant additional resources or support.

☐ There is a system in place for aggregate consultation on stressors, both potential and current, which results in leadership undertaking action planning to mitigate/prevent the stressors.

What did we learn today about recovering from burnout?

Let's say that the stress has already started to build, and you are feeling exhausted, cynical, inefficient, and worried that your performance is being affected by the stressful situations, experiences, and people you must deal with in your life. What have we learned about how we can remedy burnout and get back to feeling engaged in the tasks, roles, and responsibilities of our lives?

Yes, the removal of that project, co-worker, manager, or situation may be all that's required for your stress to go away, but that doesn't guarantee an end to the burnout symptoms. More stressful projects, co-workers, managers, and situations are potentially going to be right around the corner and spell a continuation of your burnout experience. Instead, your best action plan for recovery is to undertake strategies to help with short-term and long-term coping with stressful events and burnout.

This includes making good choices when it comes to your physical well-being. For you, this may include evaluating and changing your sleep, eating, or physical activity patterns. These physical well-being choices are not only to ensure that your body is physically healthy but also to create good habits that will help to mitigate bad ones.

This also includes looking at cognitive strategies. You can learn to recognise and acknowledge that your thoughts are just thoughts; negative thoughts are not necessarily reflections of reality. Our minds are good: They help us be aware of our environments, but we can ultimately choose when we engage in thinking on a given topic. If you don't want to be stuck ruminating over a stressful event or being anxious over what may happen tomorrow, there are exercises you can do to learn how to focus your attention on being present in the moment and not letting your mind drift over the same thoughts over and over again, as discussed in Chapter 4.

Finally, the long-term strategies for recovering from burnout are those that overcome what we understand to be the symptoms of burnout, namely, cynicism, a sense of ineffectiveness, and cognitive deficits. For you as an individual, these strategies involve changing your perspectives on the situations around you. This is best approached by talking to a trusted friend, colleague or advisor who can challenge your perceptions. After challenging your perspectives of stressful events, situations, or people, you need to begin choosing what values and goals you prioritise in your situation and which ones may be met through alternative means.

Real talk for individuals: There are times when the only solution to recovering from burnout is to cease a role, task, or responsibility. This can be because your cynicism is too far gone to take the actions to start remedying burnout, or there may be too many barriers in place that prevent you from taking the required actions to mitigate the stress. You may realise that you don't have the personal resources to fulfil the roles, tasks, or responsibilities. In these situations, seeking additional resources and support is the best course of action. If these are not available from your organisation for the specific stressor, seek support for yourself. It is not a weakness to seek support. We all need it at some point in our lives. This might be your time.

Unfortunately, leaving a role, task, or responsibility due to burnout happens, and it happens often. However, leaving a role, task, or responsibility because of burnout doesn't need to be the end of your story. The best advice for people in that situation is to begin stress risk mitigation and prevention before you begin your next role, task, or responsibility. This can be through completing the "Individual's burnout prevention task list" above.

Individual's burnout recovery task list:

☐ I have identified my physical well-being choices and patterns (e.g., sleep, eating, and exercise) and considered any choices that could be improved upon.

☐ I have undertaken practice in identifying thoughts as just thoughts, rather than necessarily reflections of reality.

☐ I have undertaken practice in learning that I can choose when to engage in thinking about a given topic.

☐ I have talked with a trusted friend, colleague, or advisor who can challenge my perceptions of stressful events, situations, or people.

☐ I have made a list of my values and goals and considered which values I can meet in my current situation, and which values I can meet through alternative means.

☐ I have sought additional support or resources from my organisation (or a third-party support organisation) to help me cope with the demands of the stressors.

What would a burnout-preventing organisation look like?

Let's say all organisational stakeholders were completely on board with making their organisation as burnout-proof as possible. Of course, it is impossible for an organisation to avoid all stressors, but there are many actions leadership can take to reduce the likelihood of their stakeholders experiencing burnout. Let's call this company "Greenham's":

Firstly, the senior managers at Greenham's are leading by example of having a healthy work-life balance by not having communications open to other stakeholders or clients outside of set work hours and encouraging employees to do the same. They are investing in forecasting and managing shareholders' expectations for what goals can realistically be achieved, given the available resources, in a given time period for the organisation so that unfounded pressures are not put on lower-level stakeholders.

Greenham's supervisors are actively consulting with subordinates to ensure they are not pressured to perform unrealistically outside their clearly defined tasks, roles, and responsibilities. Every Greenham's employee is ensuring that they understand with complete clarity what their organisational required tasks and roles are and are engaging with the relevant decision-makers to resolve any discrepancies or misalignments between resources and demands. Supervisors ensure they clearly understand each subordinate's tasks, roles, and responsibilities. Additionally, they are ensuring that the tasks are realistic and the individuals are adequately resourced in their roles to undertake the tasks.

The CEO has engaged a third party to conduct an annual consultation with all stakeholders to identify current stressors and potential risks. He ensures that this consultation is done anonymously to encourage honest feedback. After consultation, he processes the results and engages with the organisation's decision-makers to come up with actions to mitigate the stressors and potential risks.

Yes, Greenham's is a utopian organisation where everybody is looking out for the needs of others. If an organisation's decision-makers feel like this is a step too far, I believe the minimum a burnout-preventing organisation can do is put systems in place for potential risks to be identified and reasonably actioned before the stressor reaches the people they are responsible for and potentially contributes to them experiencing burnout.

Part 2
Example guide of burnout causes, symptoms, preventions, and remedies

Introduction

Part 2 of this book is intended as an example guide for preventing and remedying stressors commonly encountered by individuals working or participating in organisations and other life situations. Consistent with the thesis of this book, preventing and remedying stressors, in most cases, requires work both from the organisation and the individual.

Being a guide of nearly 100 example stressors, this is not necessarily intended to be read from top to bottom. The best use of this guide is to consider, when required, which stressors listed are closest to those being experienced and what organisational and individual remedies are suggested. The most appropriate remedies will depend on the specifics of the stressor and the individual's symptoms. If you are highly invested in preventing stress and burnout in the lives of others, there would be value in reading about the various stressors to get an idea of the potential stressors those around you may be facing.

If you are an organisation, it is recommended that this guide be used as a conversation starter if an individual is suspected or known to be experiencing stress or burnout. It would be ill-advised to ever make assumptions about the individual's symptoms, as every individual will process stressful situations differently.

If you are an individual, it is recommended that you start with identifying which individual preventions or remedies are most appropriate for you in your given situation. Only after considering your individual needs is it recommended you approach the organisation with suggestions of how they may prevent or remedy a given stressor.

As a guide to the following sections, each stressor is listed, followed by a list of an individual's potential stress/burnout symptoms, organisational prevention/remedy actions, and individual prevention/remedy actions. The stressor is an event, situation, circumstance, or stimulus that may cause individual stress and burnout. Most are intentionally broad to cover a wide range of scenarios of people's tasks, roles, and responsibilities in their work and life.

Potential individuals' symptoms: This is a non-exhaustive list of potential symptoms (an individual may feel a different symptom due to other contributing circumstances) that an individual may face when experiencing the given stressor. The lists are unsorted to not suggest one symptom is more common than another.

Organisation preventions/remedies: This is what an organisation can do to reduce the risk of the stressor affecting individuals or to stop the stressors from continuing. The lists are unsorted to not suggest one prevention/remedy is more effective than another, given every situation will be different. Multiple strategies may need to be employed or tested for efficacy.

Individual preventions/remedies: This is what an individual can do to reduce the risk of the stressor affecting themselves or to stop the stress or burnout from continuing. These lists are also unsorted to not suggest one prevention/remedy is more effective than another, given every situation will be different. Multiple strategies may need to be employed or tested for efficacy.

Being on call

Potential individuals' symptoms

Anxious at the possible extent of incoming workloads.

Mentally exhausted from the incoming workload.

Cynical at lack of support.

Physical exhaustion from lack of sleep.

Lack of social engagement due to work as a distraction.
Lack of work-life balance due to being unable to 'switch off' or not taking breaks.

Negative associations between things like the phone ringing/texts coming in, which can cause the individual to constantly be on edge.

Organisation preventions/remedies

Ensure there are adequate rest times between shifts of being on call.

Ensure that resources are available so that individuals can take required breaks during shifts.

Having additional resources ready for the individual to call upon should the need arise.

Consult on the extent of support required by the individual while on shift.

Clearly communicate the support available.

Clearly communicate what is required and the boundaries for the individual while on shift.

Provide training on best practices for being on call.

Regularly provide support check-ins on the individual to identify and remedy systematic issues.

Individual preventions/remedies
Have a clear routine, even when on call. Increase predictability as much as possible.
Follow good physical practices such as sleep and physical movement.
Learn mindfulness techniques to focus on the present moment and choose when you think about work.
Maintain clear boundaries of rest time between shifts and breaks during shifts.
Ensure support is readily available during shifts.
Bring up issues or concerns as soon as possible with supervision. Don't assume problems will improve without action.
Identify the value that you are providing others in being on call but keep your expectations realistic for what you can achieve in each shift.

Unpredictable work schedule

Potential individuals' symptoms
Anxious about when next on shift.
Lack of social engagement due to being unsure if they can book social events.
Negative associations between things like the phone ringing/ texts coming in, which can cause the individual to constantly be on edge.
Cynicism over whether shifts are being fairly distributed between workers.

Organisation preventions/remedies

Ensure there are adequate rest times between shifts.
Ensure that individuals are comfortable with the mode of communication regarding shifts.

Consult with the individual about block-out periods.

Communicate upcoming shifts in a respectful manner.
Ensure that shifts are not heavily reliant on the availability of a small set of individuals.

Communicate clear expectations of the role and the extent to which the work schedule is unpredictable.

Don't use blackmail or threats when communicating shift requirements.

Individual preventions/remedies

Set clear boundaries for modes and times of communication regarding upcoming shifts.

Set and keep clear boundaries for block-out periods of availability.

Set clear boundaries for rest time between shifts.
Ensure you are aware of the expectations of the schedule at your organisation and that it aligns with your personal values.

Identify that you are ultimately in control of your life's schedule, and you don't 'owe' anyone your resources, only what you are willing to provide.

Lack of adequate rest between shifts

Potential individuals' symptoms

Mentally exhausted from the workload.

Physically exhausted from the workload or lack of rest.

Anxiety of building exhaustion from the workload.

Cynical at lack of support/care from supervisors.

Lack of work-life balance due to being unable to 'switch off'.

A distracting preoccupation with resting.

Organisation preventions/remedies

Enforce that between-shift rest times are followed in line with required employment agreements.

Align employee expectations with the organisation's expectations of time between shifts.

Ensure that shifts are not heavily reliant on the availability of a small set of individuals.

Communicate clear expectations of the role and the extent to which there is rest between shifts.

Individual preventions/remedies

Maintain clear boundaries of the rest you are entitled to under your employment agreements.

Set and keep clear boundaries for the rest you believe you personally require between shifts.

Pre-plan activities you will undertake between concurrent shifts.

During rests, practice mindfulness to switch off from thinking about work duties.

Identify that you are ultimately in control of your life's schedule, and you don't 'owe' anyone your resources, only what you are willing to provide.

No opportunity to use leave entitlements

Potential individuals' symptoms
Cynical at lack of support/care from supervisors.
Mentally exhausted from the workload.
Physically exhausted from the workload or lack of rest.
Anxiety of building exhaustion from the workload.

Organisation preventions/remedies
Enforce that leave entitlements are used in line with required employment agreements.
As much as possible, allow for autonomy in choosing leave dates.
Ensure that resources are available to allow the individual to use their leave.
Communicate what resources are available to allow the individual to use their leave.
Ensure supervision/co-workers/others do not discourage leave entitlement.
Consult with individuals about perceived/real barriers to leave entitlements.

Individual preventions/remedies
Maintain clear boundaries of the leave you are entitled to under your employment agreements.
Identify that you are ultimately in control of your life's schedule, and you don't 'owe' anyone your resources, only what you are willing to provide.
Communicate barriers to you taking leave with your supervisor or human resource support (or even a governmental ombudsman, if available and required).

Ensure you are aware of the expectations/culture around leave at your organisation and that it aligns with your personal values.

Too much workload

Potential individuals' symptoms

Mentally exhausted from the workload.

Physically exhausted from the workload.

Anxiety of getting workload completed.

Feeling a sense of ineffectiveness about outputs.

Feeling a sense of personal failure.

Cynical at lack of support from supervisors.

Task procrastination.

Organisation preventions/remedies

Consult with individuals about workloads to locate the source/contributors to the workload and how this can be remedied.

Ensure that individuals have the resources available to deal with increased or constantly heavy workloads.

Ensure all stakeholders (including supervisors and the individual) have realistic expectations of the workloads an individual can complete.

Communicate what resources are available for the individual.

Do not encourage and reward workload outputs that are beyond the reasonable scope of an individual worker.

Ensure adequate training is available on project management.

Individual preventions/remedies
Identify the source/contributors to your workload and how work can be delegated to other parties.
Identify if there are any personal drivers to you taking on a workload that you cannot handle.
Take adequate rests and breaks, practising mindfulness to switch off from thinking about work duties.
Set strong boundaries for yourself and pre-plan other activities that will allow you to take a break from the workload.
Identify if any habits are causing you to procrastinate tasks or focus on tasks that are not contributing to reducing your workload.
Use resources and support available without personal judgement.

Not enough workload

Potential individuals' symptoms
Feeling a sense of ineffectiveness about outputs.
Feeling a sense of personal failure.
Task procrastination.

Organisation preventions/remedies
Consult with individuals about workloads to locate barriers to appropriate levels of workload. These may be systemic issues caused by inefficiencies or ineffectiveness in other areas of the organisation.
Encourage and reward the individual's initiative to improve processes and outputs.
Do not stigmatise discussion of low workloads.

Individual preventions/remedies
Identify and project-manage initiatives to improve your role
and task processes and outputs (for completion during low
workload periods).
Communicate with supervision barriers to
completing workloads.
Identify that not enough workload is not a failure of your
abilities but is highly likely to be a systematic organisational
issue that is causing barriers to your workload.

Tight deadlines/turnaround times

Potential individuals' symptoms
Mentally exhausted from the workload.

Physically exhausted from the workload.

Anxiety of getting workload completed.

Feeling a sense of ineffectiveness about outputs.

Feeling a sense of personal failure.

Cynical at lack of support from supervisors.

Task procrastination.

Feelings of resentment towards clients/supervisors to which
the deadline has been requested or promised.

Organisation preventions/remedies
Ensure all stakeholders (including supervisors and the
individual) have realistic expectations of a turnaround
time and that slack time has been included in any
promised deliveries.
Communicate what resources are available for the individual
during tight turnaround times.

Do not encourage or reward turnaround times that are beyond the reasonable scope of an individual or a project. Support individuals in keeping turnaround time boundaries with clients.

Do not suggest turnaround times to others without prior consultation with workers directly completing the project. Ensure adequate training is available on project management.

Communicate organisational expectations of turnaround times and consult on barriers that would prevent these turnaround times.

Individual preventions/remedies
Maintain clear boundaries of turnaround times of projects you are tasked with completing.

Ensure you have included slack time in any of your projected completion times.

Ensure you include an adequate allowance for rests and breaks into your projected completion times.

Identify if turnaround times are tight due to any problematic habits you have.

Identify that when others promise/ask for unreasonable turnaround times, this is often due to their lack of knowledge about the project. Educate them.

Constant fast-paced work

Potential individuals' symptoms
Mentally exhausted from the workload.
Physically exhausted from the workload.
Feeling a sense of ineffectiveness about outputs.

Feeling a sense of personal failure.

Cynical at lack of support from supervisors.

Feelings of resentment towards those who are setting the work pace, whether this be supervision or clients.

Organisation preventions/remedies

Ensure all stakeholders (including supervisors and the individual) have realistic expectations of an individual's expected work pace.

Ensure that individuals have the resources available to deal with fast-paced workloads.

Communicate what resources are available for the individual.

Ensure directly unnecessary tasks are delegated away from the individual to allow them to focus on their required tasks.

Communicate organisational expectations of work pace and consult on barriers that would prevent this work pace.

Ensure adequate training is available on efficiently completing the required tasks.

Individual preventions/remedies

Maintain clear boundaries of breaks during shifts and rests between shifts to allow recovery from work.

Physically and emotionally mutually support co-workers who are set with the same pace of work.

Identify that a pace of work that you feel exceeds your abilities is often due to a lack of knowledge about the project, in which case, educate them or another systematic issue that is beyond your control and, therefore, not a reflection on your abilities.

Identify if the work is perceived as fast-paced due to any problematic habits you have or a lack of understanding/ training on how the task is to be efficiently completed.

Long hours of work

Potential individuals' symptoms
Mentally exhausted from the workload.
Physically exhausted from the workload.
Anxiety of building exhaustion from the workload.
Feeling a sense of personal failure.
Cynical at lack of support from supervisors.
Feelings of resentment towards those who are setting/ requiring the hours, whether this be supervision or clients.

Organisation preventions/remedies
Enforce that shift breaks and rest times between shifts are followed in line with required employment agreements.
Ensure that individuals have the resources available to deal with a long shift.
Ensure adequate training is available on efficiently completing the required tasks.

Individual preventions/remedies
Maintain clear boundaries of breaks during shifts and rests between shifts to allow recovery from work.
Physically and emotionally mutually support co-workers who are set with the same lengths of work.
Identify if the work requires long hours due to any problematic habits you have or a lack of understanding/ training on how the task is to be efficiently completed.

Completing highly repetitive tasks

Potential individuals' symptoms

Mentally exhausted from work.

Physically exhausted from work.

Feeling a sense of ineffectiveness about outputs.

Feeling a sense of personal failure.

Task procrastination.

Cynical at lack of support from supervisors for requiring the repetitive tasks.

Organisation preventions/remedies

Enforce that breaks and rest times between shifts are followed in line with required employment agreements.

Ensure adequate training is available on efficiently completing the tasks.

Investigate if there are tasks that can be assigned to the individual to break up monotony.

Provide clear feedback and rewards for task completion.

Educate individuals about where their tasks fit into the wider organisation.

Ensure directly unnecessary tasks are delegated away from the individual to allow them to focus on their required tasks.

As much as possible, allow for the autonomy of break times.

As much as possible, allow for the autonomy of task completion.

Investigate if there are ways the task can be further automated to allow the individual to do other, less repetitive tasks.

Rotate workers through repetitive tasks.

Individual preventions/remedies

Maintain clear boundaries of breaks during shifts and rests between shifts to allow recovery from work.

Identify how your work provides value to others.

Identify how your work provides value to the organisation.

Physically and emotionally mutually support co-workers who are set with the same types of tasks.

Investigate how the task may be completed more efficiently to allow you to focus on other, less repetitive tasks.

Identify that the task may feel repetitive due to your competency/experience that has caused you to no longer identify anything novel in the task. Consider how you could add personal novelty to task completion if this is the case.

Completing low-skill tasks

Potential individuals' symptoms

Feeling a sense of ineffectiveness about outputs.

Feeling a sense of personal failure.

Task procrastination.

Organisation preventions/remedies

Enforce that breaks and rest times between shifts are followed in line with required employment agreements.

Ensure that the task aligns with the individual's abilities and interests.

Investigate if there are tasks that can be assigned to the individual to break up monotony.

Provide clear feedback and rewards for task completion.

Educate individuals about where their tasks fit into the wider organisation.

Investigate if there are ways the task can be further automated to allow the individual to focus on other cognitively-demanding tasks.

As much as possible, allow for the autonomy of break times.
As much as possible, allow for the autonomy of task completion.

Rotate workers through necessarily low-skill tasks.

Individual preventions/remedies
Identify and request opportunities to provide cognitive stimulation through your work.

Identify how your work provides value to others.

Identify how your work provides value to the organisation.

Physically and emotionally mutually support co-workers who are set with the same types of tasks.

Identify that the task may feel low skill due to your competency/experience that has caused you to no longer require cognitive processing to complete the task. Consider how you could add personal novelty to task completion if this is the case.

Excessive administrative/low-value tasks

Potential individuals' symptoms
Feelings of resentment towards clients/supervisors who require administrative tasks.

Feeling a sense of mistrust.

Task procrastination.

Anxiety about how administrative work may prohibit or add to other workloads.

Organisation preventions/remedies

Investigate the purpose and outputs of the administrative task to see how the task may be automated or done differently (or required at all).

Consider whether the task may be delegated or aggregated from multiple individuals to a single individual to reduce work-switching requirements.

Ensure adequate training is available on efficiently completing the required tasks.

Individual preventions/remedies

Investigate how the task may be completed more efficiently to allow you to focus on higher-value tasks.

Identify how your work provides value to others.

Identify how your work provides value to the organisation.

Identify that the low-value tasks are likely a systematic organisational issue, not a reflection of your abilities.

Identify that the low-value tasks can also likely be an issue resulting from human failure or risk reduction, not a targeted sense of mistrust.

Identify that the task may feel low value due to your competency/experience that has caused you to no longer see the benefit of completing the task. Likely, others will not have the same level of experience in your role and require your completion of administrative tasks to complete their tasks.

Varied tasks that require constant switching

Potential individuals' symptoms

Mentally exhausted from the constant switching.

Task procrastination.

Feelings of resentment towards clients/supervisors who require varied tasks.
Feeling a sense of ineffectiveness about outputs due to lack of focus.

Organisation preventions/remedies
Investigate the purpose and outputs of the tasks to see how the task may be automated or done differently (or required at all).
Consider whether the task may be delegated or aggregated from multiple individuals to a single individual to reduce work-switching requirements.
Ensure adequate training is available on efficiently completing the required tasks.
Ensure the individual clearly understands what is required of them in their role and ensure they are not adding in unnecessary tasks.

Individual preventions/remedies
Investigate how the tasks may be completed more efficiently to allow you to focus on higher-value tasks.
Investigate how the tasks may be delegated to others to allow you to focus on higher-value tasks.
Ensure you are only doing tasks that are directly required and expected of you in your role.
Project manage your role and tasks to help you better identify efficient processes.
Identify how your work provides value to others.
Identify how your work provides value to the organisation.
Group and complete similar tasks together.

Set and enforce boundaries on the amount and prioritisation of task switching throughout your shift (e.g., consider how many times your need to check your email during the day. If you're not doing an email task, turn off your email notifications).

Being constantly interrupted from tasks

Potential individuals' symptoms

Mentally exhausted from the constant switching.
Feelings of resentment towards clients/supervisors who interrupt the tasks.
Feeling a sense of ineffectiveness about outputs due to lack of focus.

Organisation preventions/remedies
As much as possible, allow for the autonomy of task completion.
Encourage and enforce meetings to be minimal and pre-planned with set times, durations, and agendas.
Identify any individuals' bad habits with communicating with others and train them on effective time management.

Individual preventions/remedies
Set and enforce boundaries on technological interruptions (e.g., If you're not doing an email task, turn off your email notifications).
Set and enforce boundaries on meetings through prior scheduling.

Identify if constant switching is due to any problematic habits you have (e.g., checking social media more than is required) and if these tasks can instead be appropriately scheduled.

Long commutes/travel required for work

Potential individuals' symptoms
Mentally exhausted from the travel.
Physically exhausted from the travel.
Feelings of resentment towards clients/supervisors who required the long commute.
Feeling a sense of ineffectiveness about work or life not completed during travel.

Organisation preventions/remedies
Investigate the purpose of travel/commute and identify where travel may be reduced.
Consult with the individual on initiatives that could add comfort to their travel (e.g., going with a co-worker, allowing stipends).
Ensure all stakeholders have reasonable expectations for performance expectations around travel (e.g., not expecting workers to necessarily start immediately after arrival at work).

Individual preventions/remedies
Identify how the travel to your work provides value to others.
Identify how the travel to your work provides value to the organisation.
Investigate and request reasonable initiatives that will add comfort to your travel.

Investigate activities that will add value to your travel. Practice mindfulness or use distracting activities so that you are not focused on work for the duration of your travel.

Physical and mental demand

Physically demanding work

Potential individuals' symptoms

Physically exhausted.

Mentally exhausted due to lack of rest.

Feelings of resentment towards clients/supervisors who require the work.

Anxiety of building exhaustion.

Lack of work-life balance due to rest needs.

Organisation preventions/remedies

Enforce that breaks and rest times between shifts are followed in line with required employment agreements.

Ensure that the task is in line with the individual's physical abilities.

Ensure adequate training is available on efficiently and safely completing the required tasks.

Ensure the individual is efficiently and safely completing the required tasks.

Ensure the individual clearly understands what physical tasks are required of them and what resources are available to help them.

Ensure there are appropriate resources (e.g., plentiful and well-maintained) to help the individual complete the task.

Individual preventions/remedies

Maintain clear boundaries of breaks during shifts and rests between shifts to allow recovery from work.

Identify that you are ultimately in control of your body, and you don't need to do anything physical that is beyond your skills or resources, only what you are willing to provide. You don't need to prove anything to anyone.

Pursue training to learn how to complete the task safely and efficiently.

Use or request the resources and support available to complete the tasks safely and efficiently.

Mentally demanding work

Potential individuals' symptoms

Mentally exhausted due to focus.

Feeling a sense of ineffectiveness when not able to easily propose solutions to problems.

Feelings of resentment towards clients/supervisors who require the work.

Anxiety of not being able to complete the task to own/others perceived levels of requirements.

Organisation preventions/remedies

Enforce that breaks and rest times between shifts are followed in line with required employment agreements.

Ensure that the task is in line with the individual's learned abilities.

Ensure adequate training is available on efficiently completing the required tasks.

Ensure the individual is not completing the required tasks beyond what is reasonably required.

Ensure the individual clearly understands what mental tasks are required of them and what resources are available to help them.

Ensure there are appropriate resources (e.g., others more experienced) to help the individual complete the task.

Do not stigmatise individuals asking for help.

Do not add unnecessary tasks that will distract the individual, both during and after the mentally demanding task.

Individual preventions/remedies
Maintain clear boundaries of breaks during shifts and rests between shifts to allow recovery from work.

Pursue training to learn how to efficiently complete the task. Use or request the resources and support available to efficiently complete the tasks.

Identify that your successes and failures should not be compared to others but only to what you can achieve, given your prior training, knowledge, and experience. You don't need to prove anything to anyone.

Identify that it is not a failure to ask for help and instead is an opportunity to learn.

Pre-plan activities or practice mindfulness to allow you to switch off from work during breaks.

High concentration work

Potential individuals' symptoms
Mentally exhausted due to focus.
Physically exhausted due to tensing, maintaining the same position for a long time etc.

Anxiety of not being able to complete the task to own/others perceived levels of requirements.

Feelings of resentment towards clients/supervisors who require the work.

Anxiety of next high-concentration task.

Organisation preventions/remedies
Enforce that breaks and rest times between shifts are followed in line with required employment agreements.
Ensure that the task is in line with the individual's learned abilities.
Ensure adequate training is available on efficiently completing the required tasks.
Ensure that the individual is appropriately resourced to efficiently complete their tasks.
Do not stigmatise individuals asking for help.
Do not add unnecessary tasks that will distract the individual, both during and after the mentally demanding task.

Individual preventions/remedies
Maintain clear boundaries of breaks during shifts and rests between shifts to allow recovery from work.
Pursue training to learn how to efficiently complete the task.
Use or request the resources and support available to efficiently complete the tasks.
Identify that your successes and failures should not be compared to others but only to what you can achieve, given your prior training, knowledge, and experience. You don't need to prove anything to anyone.

Identify that it is not a failure to ask for help and instead is an opportunity to learn.

Pre-plan activities or practice mindfulness to allow you to switch off from work during breaks.

Displaying false emotions as part of the job

Potential individuals' symptoms
Mentally exhausted due to empathy and concentration requirements.

Physically exhausted due to tensing, maintaining the same position for a long time etc.

Feelings of resentment towards clients/supervisors who require the work.

Organisation preventions/remedies
Ensure that individuals have access to emotional support to process their genuine emotions.

Rotate workers through necessarily high empathy tasks.
Ensure that individuals have training on empathy and the limits/expectations of their roles and tasks.

As much as possible, allow for the autonomy of task completion.

Check in with individuals regularly to non-judgementally allow individuals to express their genuine emotions in a safe environment.

Ensure individuals know they have support resources when they do not feel they can sustain the required emotion of the task.

Ensure individuals have a safe space they can go to after engaging in any tasks that cause them to feel any strong, negative emotions.

Ensure individuals have the appropriate temperament to engage in a given task. This should be periodically assessed as it may change over time.

Ensure individuals have aligned expectations of the required tasks in the role and how it may emotionally affect them.

Individual preventions/remedies
Identify and learn that you can choose when you express a given emotion, and your emotions don't need to be dictated by the emotions or behaviour of another person.

Emotionally mutually support others who are completing similar tasks.

Ensure that you rest and process your own emotions in a safe environment after engaging in any tasks that cause you to feel any strong, negative emotions.

Identify that the tasks you are required to do fit with your abilities to process the relevant emotions, given your own life experiences. Not being able to emotionally handle a certain situation or circumstance should not be seen as a personal failure but rather a result of your lived experiences.

Seek emotional support (informal or formal) if you feel you are unable to process a given emotion or circumstance.

Responding/Dealing with emotional situations

Potential individuals' symptoms
Mentally exhausted due to empathy and concentration requirements.

Physically exhausted due to tensing, maintaining the same position for a long time etc.

Feelings of resentment towards clients/supervisors who caused/required the emotional situation.

Anxiety of the next highly emotional situation.

Organisation preventions/remedies
Ensure that individuals have access to emotional support to process their reactions, emotions, and feelings.
Ensure that individuals have training on empathy and the limits/expectations of their roles and tasks.
As much as possible, allow for the autonomy of task completion.
Check in with individuals regularly to non-judgementally allow individuals to express their genuine emotions in a safe environment.
Ensure individuals have a safe space they can go to after engaging in any tasks that cause them to feel any strong, negative emotions.
Ensure individuals have the appropriate temperament to engage in a given task. This should be periodically assessed as it may change over time.
Ensure individuals have aligned expectations of the required tasks in the role and how it may emotionally affect them.

Individual preventions/remedies
Identify and learn that you can choose when you express a given emotion, and your emotions don't need to be dictated by the emotions or behaviour of another person.
Identify how your work provides value to others.
Emotionally mutually support others who are completing similar tasks.
Ensure that you rest and process your own emotions in a safe environment after engaging in any tasks that cause you to feel any strong, negative emotions.

Identify that the tasks you are required to do fit with your abilities to process the relevant emotions, given your own life experiences. Not being able to emotionally handle a certain situation or circumstance should not be seen as a personal failure but rather a result of your lived experiences.

Seek informal emotional or formal mental health support if you feel you are unable to process a given emotion or circumstance.

Exposed to traumatic materials in the course of work

Potential individuals' symptoms
Mentally exhausted due to inability to process through materials, intrusive thoughts.

Physically exhausted due to tensing, lack of sleep etc.
Feelings of resentment towards clients/supervisors who caused/required the emotional situation.

Anxiety of next traumatic materials.

Emotionally triggered by reminders.

Lack of social connection due to withdrawal/feelings of isolation.

Organisation preventions/remedies
Ensure that a minimum number of individuals are exposed to traumatic materials.

Ensure all materials (e.g., files) are clearly marked and appropriately labelled as containing potentially traumatic materials. Ensure these are protected from accidental viewings (e.g., password protected).

Rotate workers through these tasks to minimise the quantity of exposure.

Ensure individuals have a safe space they can go to after engaging in any tasks that cause them to feel any strong, negative emotions.

Ensure individuals have the appropriate temperament to engage in a given task. This should be periodically assessed as it may change over time.

Ensure individuals have aligned expectations of the required tasks in the role and how it may emotionally affect them.

Regularly check in with individuals exposed and monitor for changes in behaviours for further support requirements.

Individual preventions/remedies

Learn to recognise and validate your own emotions.

Practice mindfulness to help you rest from processing materials.

Identify how your work provides value to others.

Emotionally mutually support others who are completing similar tasks.

Identify that the tasks you are required to do fit with your abilities to process the relevant emotions, given your own life experiences. Not being able to emotionally handle a certain situation or circumstance should not be seen as a personal failure but rather a result of your lived experiences.

Seek training on trauma to learn how it may affect you and how you can work through it.

Seek informal emotional or formal mental health support if you feel you are unable to process a given emotion or circumstance.

High-risk tasks

Potential individuals' symptoms

Mentally exhausted due to high concentration.

Physically exhausted due to tensing, maintaining a position for an extended period of time, energy expenditure etc.

Anxiety of next high-risk task.

Anxiety of not being able to complete the task to own/others perceived levels of requirements.

Organisation preventions/remedies

Enforce that breaks and rest times between shifts are followed in line with required employment agreements.

Ensure that the task is in line with the individual's learned abilities.

Ensure adequate training is available on efficiently completing the required tasks.

Ensure that the individual is appropriately resourced to efficiently complete their tasks.

Do not stigmatise individuals asking for help.

Clearly communicate to individuals the expectations of task completion.

Ensure all stakeholders are aware of and accept the risks before requiring the individual to complete the task.

Do not add unnecessary tasks that will add distractions to the individual, both during and after the high-risk task.

Individual preventions/remedies

Maintain clear boundaries of breaks during shifts and rests between shifts to allow recovery from tasks.

Identify that your successes and failures should not be compared to others but only to what you can achieve, given your prior training, knowledge, and experience. You don't need to prove anything to anyone.

Identify that it is not a failure to ask for help and instead is an opportunity to learn.

Use or request the resources and support available to efficiently complete the tasks.

Lack of error-checking support

Potential individuals' symptoms

Mentally exhausted due to high concentration.

Anxiety of making mistakes.

Anxiety of not being able to complete the task to own/others perceived levels of requirements.

Organisation preventions/remedies

Consult with individuals about what error-checking mechanisms need to be implemented.

Provide the appropriate error-checking resources.

Ensure adequate training is available to give the individual confidence for completing the required tasks.

Do not stigmatise individuals asking for help.

Ensure that the requirements of the task are clearly communicated so the individual knows where to appropriately focus their time and effort.

Individual preventions/remedies
Identify that your successes and failures should not be compared to others but only to what you can achieve given your prior training, knowledge, and experience. You don't need to prove anything to anyone.

Use or request the resources and support available to gain confidence when completing the task.

Ask for task clarifications from other stakeholders early in the project to avoid errors that could have been avoided with more information.

High compliance requirements for routine tasks

Potential individuals' symptoms
Feelings of resentment towards clients/supervisors who require high compliance.

Anxiety of discipline/reprimand for missing a compliance step.

Organisation preventions/remedies
Investigate the purpose and outputs of the compliance requirements to see how the task may be automated or done differently (or required at all).

Ensure adequate training is available on efficiently completing the required compliance tasks.

Support individuals in setting boundaries for clients who have unreasonable compliance requirements.

Individual preventions/remedies
Investigate how the task may be completed more efficiently to allow you to focus on higher-value tasks.

Identify how your work provides value to others.

Identify how your work provides value to the organisation.

Identify that the compliance tasks are likely a systematic organisational issue, not a reflection of your abilities.

Identify that the compliance tasks can also likely be an issue resulting from human failure or risk reduction, not a targeted sense of mistrust.

Identify that the task may feel like a hassle due to your competency/experience which has caused you to no longer see the benefit of completing that type of compliance task.

Lack of autonomy in decision making

Potential individuals' symptoms
Feelings of resentment towards clients/supervisors who demand high control.

Feeling a sense of ineffectiveness about work when they can see a better solution.

Organisation preventions/remedies
Ensure that the individual's level of autonomy matches their level of skill.

Ensure that all stakeholders clearly understand their roles and tasks, and where they are and are not able to be autonomous in their decision-making.

Clearly set expectations early for the levels of autonomy available in the task/role/organisational responsibilities.

Identify areas where the individual can have increased autonomy.

Individual preventions/remedies
Identify that people have different experiences, knowledge, and skills. This will shape their views on how solutions may be effective or ineffective.
Identify areas you can ensure autonomy, even if it's not in the optimal areas where you see different solutions are required.
Ensure you have a clear understanding and expectations for the areas in which you can have autonomy.

Lack of autonomy in task completion methods

Potential individuals' symptoms
Feelings of resentment towards clients/supervisors who demand high control.
Feeling a sense of ineffectiveness about tasks when they can see a better solution.

Organisation preventions/remedies
Ensure that the individual's level of autonomy matches their level of skill.
Ensure that all stakeholders clearly understand their roles and tasks, and where they are and are not able to be autonomous in the way they complete their tasks.
Clearly set expectations early for the levels of autonomy available in the task/role/organisational responsibilities.
Clearly communicate why a given task completion method is required.
Identify areas where the individual can have increased autonomy.

Individual preventions/remedies
Identify that people have different experiences, knowledge, and skills. This will shape their views on how methods may be effective or ineffective.

Identify if there are areas you can ensure autonomy, even if it's not in the optimal areas you see different solutions are required.

Ensure you have a clear understanding and expectations for the areas in which you can have autonomy.

Clearly communicate why you can see a task completion method as being optimal over another.

Lack of control over breaks/moving away from tasks

Potential individuals' symptoms
Feelings of resentment towards clients/supervisors who demand high control.

Anxiety of building exhaustion from the workload.

Cynical at lack of support/care from supervisors.

A distracting preoccupation with resting.

Organisation preventions/remedies
Clearly set expectations early for the levels of autonomy available for taking breaks.

Consult with individuals around if there are specific times they prefer their breaks.

Clearly communicate why there are specific break times required.

Identify areas where the individual can have increased autonomy.

Encourage supervisors to treat individuals with respect and decency.
Have slack resources available to handle unforeseen circumstances in which an individual needs to take an unplanned break.

Individual preventions/remedies
Identify if there are areas you can increase autonomy around your breaks (e.g., choosing a location).
Ensure you have a clear understanding and expectations for the areas in which you can have autonomy.
Identify that a lack of autonomy over breaks is likely a systematic organisational issue that is putting pressure on your supervisor to exert control over breaks.

Lack of control over the physical environment

Potential individuals' symptoms
Feelings of resentment towards clients/supervisors who demand work in a given physical environment.
Anxiety of physical exhaustion or injury from work.
Cynical at lack of support/care from supervisors.
A distracting preoccupation with working in a different environment.
Physical discomfort.
Interpersonal conflicts over the environment.
Lower productivity.

Organisation preventions/remedies
Clearly set expectations early for the work physical environment.

Periodically consult with individuals about issues caused by the physical environment.

Periodically consult with individuals about if any changes to the physical environment would improve their time completing the work.

Ensure adequate training is available on efficiently completing tasks in the required environment.

Provide the appropriate support and resources for individuals in the environment.

Individual preventions/remedies
Identify if there are areas you can increase autonomy around your working environment (e.g., choosing a different desk, introducing things to make your work in the environment more comfortable).

Clearly communicate any pressing issues of the environment that you think may have safety or task efficiency implications.

Request any support or resources that would improve your time working in the environment.

Lack of control over job outcomes

Potential individuals' symptoms
Feeling a sense of ineffectiveness.

Anxiety of not being able to complete the task to own/others perceived levels of requirements.

Anxiety of discipline/reprimand/judgement for outcomes.

Task procrastination.

Organisation preventions/remedies
Provide the support and resources for individuals
to understand the extent to which they have control
over outcomes.
Consult with individuals about where they feel there is a lack
of control over outcomes and reassure or correct individuals
as required.
Clearly set expectations early for the extent to which the
individual will have control over the outcomes.

Individual preventions/remedies
Identify that your successes and failures are always
contributed to by factors beyond your control. They are
not necessarily a reflection of your skills, knowledge,
or experience.
Physically and emotionally mutually support co-workers who
are set with similar tasks.
Seek informal emotional or formal mental health support if
you feel you are unable to process the extent of your control
in a situation.

Role and task structure

No clear career progression

Potential individuals' symptoms

Feeling down about past/current career choices.

Task procrastination.

Lower productivity.

Feelings of resentment towards others with
career progression.

Anxiety about future career prospects.

Anxiety about judgements from other people.

A sense of ineffectiveness.

A distracting preoccupation with careers (e.g., job searching).

Organisation preventions/remedies

Clearly set expectations early for the extent to which there is
career progression available in the role and organisation.
Offer upskill training where available, even if it is to a
different career within the organisation.
Offer increased responsibilities that align with the
individual's skills and experience.

Individual preventions/remedies

Identify what your personal career goals are.
Identify how your personal values align with the
opportunities available within the given organisation.
Seek out opportunities to take on tasks and responsibilities
that align with your goals.
Discuss with other stakeholders about opportunities or gaps
you could see filled with a career progression path.

Clearly communicate to supervisors your career goals.
Seek out training and professional development
opportunities to upskill towards your career goals.
Pursue short-term activities that help fulfil some
of your work desires (e.g., volunteer in a charity or
sports organisation)

Fear of redundancy

Potential individuals' symptoms
Feeling down about past/current career choices.
Anxiety about future life prospects.
Anxiety about future career prospects.
Anxiety about judgements from other people.
A sense of ineffectiveness.
A distracting preoccupation with job searching.
Physically exhausted due to tensing, lack of sleep etc.
Mentally exhausted.

Organisation preventions/remedies
Clearly regularly communicate any necessary updates to
individual's roles as soon as information is confirmed.
Do not encourage or engage in gossip regarding
individuals' roles.
Consult with the individual and engage/answer any
questions they have about their role.

Individual preventions/remedies
Ask for clarification from other decision-making
stakeholders regarding the information you suspect about
the future of your role.

Do not engage in gossip about the future of your or others' roles.

Identify that the future of your role in an organisation is always contributed to by factors beyond your control. Redundancy is not necessarily a reflection of your skills, knowledge, or experience.

During rests, practice mindfulness to switch off from thinking about your career.

Talk with a trusted advisor or career consultant to make a contingency plan for if there is redundancy. This will give you security that there is a plan B.

Lack of consultation in changes for their role or tasks

Potential individuals' symptoms
Feelings of resentment towards supervisors who changed task/role requirements.

A sense of ineffectiveness.

Feeling down about past/current career choices.

Anxiety of future changes.

Feeling a sense of mistrust.

Task procrastination.

Organisation preventions/remedies
Clearly regularly communicate any necessary updates to individual's roles as soon as information is confirmed.

Consult with the individual and engage/answer any questions they have about their role.

Identify areas where changes can be proposed in consultation with the individual.

Ensure adequate training, support and resources are immediately available for new areas of responsibility. Communicate the changes with respect and dignity.

Individual preventions/remedies
Identify that the functions of your role in an organisation are always contributed to by factors beyond your control. Changes are not necessarily a reflection of your skills, knowledge, or experience.
Engage with decision-makers by providing new information where you believe a change would be detrimental to the success of the organisation.
Identify how the changes align with your career goals, or if the changes were just unexpected.

Unclear roles and responsibilities

Potential individuals' symptoms
Feelings of resentment towards supervisors who set task/role requirements.
A sense of ineffectiveness.
Anxiety of not being able to complete the task to own/others perceived levels of requirements.
Anxiety of discipline/reprimand/judgement for outcomes.
Task procrastination.
Mentally exhausted due to high concentration and guessing.

Organisation preventions/remedies
Clearly set and communicate every individual's roles, tasks and responsibilities.

Consult with the individual and engage/answer any questions they have about their role.
Ensure adequate training, support and resources is available for the given role.
Provide an avenue of convenient, non-judgemental clarifications to an individual's role.

Individual preventions/remedies
Ask for clarification from supervision for the information you need to complete your role and responsibilities.
Write down what you believe your roles and responsibilities to be and ask the supervisor to sign it.
Keep to the boundaries of the scope of your role and only engage with responsibilities outside your role after further negotiation or discussion.
Identify that every role will have areas of ambiguity (which is not ideal) and is contributed to by factors beyond your control. Identify if a responsibility is in line with what a reasonable person would expect someone in your role to do.

Frequently changing roles and responsibilities

Potential individuals' symptoms
Feelings of resentment towards supervisors who set task/role requirements.
A sense of ineffectiveness.
Anxiety of not being able to complete the task to own/others perceived levels of requirements.
Anxiety of discipline/reprimand/judgement for outcomes.
Task procrastination.
Mentally exhausted due to high concentration and guessing.

Organisation preventions/remedies
Identify sources of frequent role and responsibilities changes and communicate this to the individual, including identifying actions that will help minimise the changes in the future.
Ensure adequate training, support and resources are immediately available for new areas of responsibility.
Consult with the individual and engage/answer any questions they have about their role.
Provide an avenue of convenient, non-judgemental clarifications to an individual's role.

Individual preventions/remedies
Ask for clarification from supervision for the information you need to complete your role and responsibilities.
Identify that every role will have areas of ambiguity (which is not ideal) and is contributed to by factors beyond your control.
Identify how the changes align with your career goals, or if the changes were just unexpected.

Unclear organisational priorities

Potential individuals' symptoms
Feelings of resentment towards leaders who are perceived to not have priorities.
Anxiety of not being able to complete the task to own/others perceived levels of requirements.
Anxiety of discipline/reprimand/judgement for outcomes.
Task procrastination.
Mentally exhausted due to high concentration and guessing.

Organisation preventions/remedies
Clearly set and communicate every organisational priority
and how it relates to each individual's roles, tasks,
and responsibilities.
Consult with each individual and engage/answer any
questions they have about how their role fits into the
organisational priorities.
Provide an avenue of convenient, non-judgemental
clarification for organisational priorities.
If the organisational priorities are unclear or there is a
misunderstanding, do not discipline/reprimand/judge
individuals if they are completing any tasks which contribute
to the success of the organisation.

Individual preventions/remedies
Ask for clarification from leadership regarding the
organisational priorities and how they affect what you
prioritise in your role and responsibilities.
Identify that organisational priorities may change depending
on changing external factors/influence of decision-maker
stakeholder priorities. If you are unable to identify or no one
can communicate the organisational priorities, your best
course of action is to focus on what you perceive to be the
highest priority tasks for the growth of the organisation. You
should not be faulted for this approach.

Mismatched expectations of the job

Potential individuals' symptoms
Feelings of resentment towards leadership who
communicated a given job profile.
Task procrastination.

Organisation preventions/remedies
Clearly set and communicate every role and responsibility and ensure that all stakeholders are aware of
this information.
Be vigilant and transparent in providing job details to
potential candidates.
Admit fault in errors in communicating job expectations and negotiate the fit of the accurate job description with
the individual.

Individual preventions/remedies
Ask for clarification from supervision for the information you need to complete your role and responsibilities.
Write down what you believe your roles and responsibilities to be and ask the supervisor to sign it.
Identify how the accurate job information aligns with your career goals.

Support and resources

Lack of resources to complete tasks

Potential individuals' symptoms
Feelings of resentment towards supervision for not
providing resources.
Anxiety of not being able to complete the task to own/others
perceived levels of requirements.
Anxiety of discipline/reprimand/judgement for outcomes.
Mentally exhausted due to extra work to meet
task requirements.
Physically exhausted due to extra work to meet
task requirements.
Lower productivity.

Organisation preventions/remedies
Consult with the individual to ensure that necessary
resources are available for the tasks to be completed.
Ensure there are resources available for when there are
unexpected demands/barriers to task completion.
Provide adequate training (e.g., project management) to
help the individual better predict resource needs to complete
their tasks.

Individual preventions/remedies
Clearly communicate with supervisors if there are any/
predicted shortfalls of resources available to complete tasks.
Identify that resource availability is dependent on many
factors and is not necessarily a reflection of your knowledge,
skill, or expertise.

Use/Learn project management to have a better awareness of upcoming/current resource needs.

Inadequate systems required for tasks

Potential individuals' symptoms
Feelings of resentment towards supervision for not providing adequate systems.
Anxiety of not being able to complete the task to own/others perceived levels of requirements.
Anxiety of discipline/reprimand/judgement for outcomes.
Mentally exhausted due to extra work to meet task requirements.
Physically exhausted due to extra work to meet task requirements.
Task procrastination.
A sense of inefficacy.

Organisation preventions/remedies
Consult with the individual to ensure that necessary systems are available for the tasks to be completed.
Provide adequate training to help the individual understand how to use current systems efficiently and correctly.
Encourage individuals to come up with solutions/share their experience of other systems that they believe would be better optimised for helping the organisation reach its goals.

Individual preventions/remedies
Identify that there are different systems that can have similar outcomes, and your sense of a system inadequacy may be from inexperience/non-use of a given specific system.

Request/use training on the given system before bringing forth any suggestions for system optimisation.
Present system problems with solutions to decision-makers in the context of how the system optimisation would better suit the goals of the organisation.

Supervision unavailable for support

Potential individuals' symptoms
Feelings of resentment towards supervision for not being available.
Anxiety of not being able to complete the task to supervision's specific requirements.
Anxiety of discipline/reprimand/judgement for outcomes.
A sense of inefficacy.
Mentally exhausted due to high concentration and guessing.

Organisation preventions/remedies
Ensure that expectations are clearly communicated with individuals regarding how much contact they should expect from supervision.
Regularly consult with the individual about if there are specific issues that they would like supervision to help with.
Consider providing the individual with an alternative avenue of supervision/support for a period of time.
Identify how supervision would benefit the organisation.

Individual preventions/remedies
Identify that supervisors have their own motivations and goals, and those motivations may be at odds with your own goals.

Consult with the supervisor directly to organise a periodic check-in time.

Discuss with your supervisor the benefits to the organisation of being provided support.

Emotionally mutually support others who are in a similar situation.

Supervision unwilling to give support

Potential individuals' symptoms

Feelings of resentment towards supervision for not being willing to give support.

Anxiety of not being able to complete the task to supervision's specific requirements.

Anxiety of discipline/reprimand/judgement for outcomes.

A sense of inefficacy.

Reduced confidence.

Mentally exhausted due to high concentration and guessing.

Organisation preventions/remedies

Ensure that expectations are clearly communicated with individuals regarding how much contact they should expect from supervision.

Identify how support fits into the roles and responsibilities of the supervisor.

Provide 3rd party mediation between the supervisor and the individual if there are any unresolved conflicts or miscommunications.

Individual preventions/remedies

Identify that supervisors have their own motivations and goals, and those motivations may be at odds with your own goals. You are ultimately not responsible for the behaviours of other people; you can only influence them.

Clearly communicate with the supervisor how their lack of support is causing you barriers in your role and responsibilities. Identify that it may be a case of misunderstanding or miscommunication about the support required.

Consult with leadership about how your supervisor's roles and responsibilities align with providing you support. Ask for their support in seeking supervision.

Emotionally mutually support others who are in a similar situation.

During rests, practice mindfulness to switch off from thinking about your supervisor.

Mutual support is discouraged

Potential individuals' symptoms

Feelings of resentment towards supervision for not allowing mutual support.

Feelings of isolation.

Anxiety of being compared to others.

Anxiety of being discussed behind one's back.

Organisation preventions/remedies

Identify the extent to which the goals of the organisation would be hindered due to mutual support.

Consult with the individual specific areas in which they would like support and provide appropriate resources to meet that support (e.g., advisory, counselling).

Identify that mutual support is important for individuals. Consider whether there was a historical incident (e.g., gossip, slander of a supervisor, unionisation discussion) that led to mutual support being discouraged and consider the extent to which the reaction from certain stakeholders outweighed the threats and opportunities that support can bring.

Individual preventions/remedies
Identify what support you require and seek out alternative avenues than those at work (e.g., a trusted friend, family member or even formal counselling).

Communicate barriers to mutual support with your supervisor or human resource support.

If mutual support is discouraged at the workplace, consider how colleagues can support each other outside of work hours or through alternative modes of communication.

Mutual support is unavailable

Potential individuals' symptoms
Feelings of isolation.

Anxiety of being compared to others.

Anxiety of being discussed behind one's back.

Reduced confidence.

Organisation preventions/remedies
Identify opportunities for the individual to receive the support they require (e.g., advisory, counselling).

Consider the extent to which the individual may be put on projects with other people, to provide them mutual support.

Individual preventions/remedies
Identify what support you require and seek out alternative avenues than those at work (e.g., a trusted friend, family member or even formal counselling).
Communicate your desire for mutual support with your supervisor or human resource support.
If mutual support is unavailable for your direct projects, consider how colleagues can support each other outside of work hours or through alternative modes of communication.

Support is unempathetic

Potential individuals' symptoms
Feelings of resentment towards unempathetic supervision.
Feelings of isolation.
A sense of inefficacy.
Reduced confidence.
Mentally exhausted due to certain issues not being resolved.

Organisation preventions/remedies
Identify the sources of unempathetic support (remember, it might be you as well) and provide adequate training on how to provide empathetic support.
Consult with the individual for support that they do find empathetic or listens well and consider how the individual may work together with that support for solutions to given issues.

Individual preventions/remedies
Identify alternative avenues of empathetic support than
those at work (e.g., a trusted friend, family member or even
formal counselling).
Communicate issues where you feel you are not being
heard or empathised with, with your supervisor or human
resource support.
Emotionally mutually support others who are facing
similar issues.

Lack of training and personal development opportunities

Potential individuals' symptoms
Feeling down about past/current career choices.
Feelings of resentment towards supervision for not
providing training.
Task procrastination.
Lower productivity.
Anxiety about future career prospects.
Anxiety about judgements from other people.
A sense of ineffectiveness.
Anxiety of not being able to complete the task to own/others
perceived levels of requirements.

Organisation preventions/remedies
Consult with the individual, without judgement, for areas
where they desire training and personal development.
Identify how training would be an investment for the future
of the business.

Identify how training would be in-line with optimising the individual's roles and responsibilities.

Individual preventions/remedies
When requesting training, take the initiative to pre-identify the training opportunities you wish to pursue.
Identify how the training or personal development would fit into your clearly defined organisational roles and tasks and communicate this to your supervisor.
Identify that training availability is likely dependent on a wide scope of factors that are ultimately outside your control. If you have made a reasonable effort to pursue the training, but it remains unavailable, consider that your success or failures in each avenue of skills is not your ultimate responsibility, but that of the organisation.

Access barriers to resources for completing tasks

Potential individuals' symptoms
Feelings of resentment towards those perceived to have created the barriers.

Task procrastination.

Lower productivity.

Anxiety about judgements from other people.

A sense of ineffectiveness.

Anxiety of not being able to complete the task to own/others perceived levels of requirements.

Organisation preventions/remedies
Periodically consult with individuals about barriers that they believe exist now, or may exist in the future, for them completing their tasks (remember, you may also be a perceived barrier).
Consult with the individuals about the support, resources or training required to overcome the access barrier.
Consult with individuals on the extent to which access barriers may be reduced through increased resource quantity or convenience.
Provide the necessary improvements to decrease access barriers in-line with the organisation's goals.

Individual preventions/remedies
Communicate access barriers as soon as they are apparent, or perceived to be coming, with your supervisor or human resource support, along with proposed solutions that fit with the goals of the organisation.
Identify that access barriers may not necessarily be caused by the decisions of one individual, but rather may be the result of a systematic organisational issue.
Identify that resource availability and access is likely dependant on a wide scope of factors that are ultimately outside your control. If you have made a reasonable effort to pursue decreasing the access barriers, but they remain, consider that your success or failures for the given tasks is not your ultimate responsibility, but that of the organisation.

Working with failing equipment

Potential individuals' symptoms
Feelings of resentment towards those perceived to have not maintained the equipment or invested the resources to do so.
Lower productivity.
Anxiety about judgements from other people.
A sense of ineffectiveness.
Anxiety of not being able to complete the task to own/others perceived levels of requirements.

Organisation preventions/remedies
Periodically consult with individuals about equipment failures that they believe exist now, or may exist in the future, for them completing their tasks.
Consult with the individuals about the support, resources or training required to continue their given tasks.
Provide the appropriate support and resources for individuals to be able to optimally complete their roles and tasks.

Individual preventions/remedies
Communicate equipment issues as soon as they are apparent, or perceived to be coming, with your supervisor, along with proposed solutions that fit with the goals of the organisation.
Identify that equipment issues may not necessarily be caused by the decisions of one individual, but rather may be the result of a systematic organisational issue.

Identify that resource availability and maintenance are likely dependent on a wide scope of factors that are ultimately outside your control. If you have made a reasonable effort to pursue decreasing the access barriers, but they remain, consider that your success or failures for the given tasks is not your ultimate responsibility, but that of the organisation.

Communication and feedback

Insufficient/unclear information

Potential individuals' symptoms
Feelings of resentment towards those perceived as not providing the necessary information.

Task procrastination.

Lower productivity.

Anxiety about judgements from other people.

A sense of ineffectiveness.

Anxiety of not being able to complete the task to own/others perceived levels of requirements.

Organisation preventions/remedies
Regularly consult with individuals, without judgement, for information that they perceive to be insufficient or unclear and any perceived barriers to information.

Record information in written documents that are reasonably accessible, convenient, and readable. Ensure all stakeholders have knowledge of and understand the written documents.

Identify that information that is clear or sufficient to a given stakeholder may not be to another given differences in knowledge, skills, and experience. Ensure that information is provided for the lowest necessary common denominator.

Individual preventions/remedies
Communicate information issues to your supervisor or human resource support.

Identify that a lack of information may be due to a systematic organisational issue, and not the direct incompetence or unwillingness of a given individual.

Read through any relevant written documentation and note any areas where you perceive there is a lack of information so that discussion on this topic can directly speak to the information available.

Identify that information availability is likely dependent on a wide scope of factors that are ultimately outside your control. If you have made a reasonable effort to pursue information, but you remain without, consider that your success or failures for the given roles or tasks is not your ultimate responsibility, but that of the organisation.

Contradictory information

Potential individuals' symptoms
Feelings of resentment towards those perceived as giving contradictory information.

Task procrastination.

Lower productivity.

Anxiety about judgements from other people.

A sense of ineffectiveness.

Anxiety of not being able to complete the task to own/others perceived levels of requirements.

Increased gossip.

Organisation preventions/remedies
Regularly consult with individuals, without judgement, for information that they perceive to be contradictory and any perceived sources of this contradictory information (remember, this may include you).

146

Record information in written documents that are reasonably accessible, convenient, and readable. Ensure all stakeholders have knowledge of, understand and have agreement on the meaning of the written documents. Identify that information (and especially organisational goals) may be interpreted differently between stakeholders given differences of knowledge, skills, and experience. Ensure that the information is directly communicated to the necessary individuals from the individual who has been given the clearly defined task of deciding and disseminating the given necessary information.

Individual preventions/remedies
Communicate information issues to your supervisor or human resource support.
Identify that contradictory information may be due to a systematic organisational issue, and not the direct incompetence or unwillingness of a given individual.
Read through any relevant written documentation and note any areas where you perceive there is contradictory information so that discussion on this topic can directly speak to the information available.
Identify that information accuracy is dependent on a wide scope of factors that are ultimately outside your control. If you have made a reasonable effort to pursue accurate information, but you remain without, consider that your success or failures for the given roles or tasks is not your ultimate responsibility, but that of the organisation and the stakeholder who has been given the clearly defined task of deciding and disseminating the given necessary information

Lack of consultation to stakeholders

Potential individuals' symptoms
Feelings of resentment towards those perceived as making decisions without consultation.

Anxiety about judgements from other people.

A sense of ineffectiveness.

Task procrastination.

Lower productivity.

Organisation preventions/remedies
Regularly communicate with the individual about any changes and why they are being made with/without consultation, being respectful of the individual's knowledge, skills, and experience.

Identify areas of decisions that can be done in consultation with the individual.

Empower the individual to be able to provide all feedback on decisions and discourse with the individual on this feedback. Ensure this discussion is always in the context of clearly defined and mutually understood tasks, roles, responsibilities, and the organisation's goals.

Individual preventions/remedies
Identify that a lack of consultation on a decision that you believe that you have the necessary knowledge, skills, and experience to make an informed contribution to may not be from a lack of respect, but rather the decision maker's lack of knowledge of your availability, interest, or investment in the decision.

Clearly and respectfully communicate your feedback on a given issue, staying in the context of how it would affect your own clearly defined tasks, roles and responsibilities and the organisation's goals. Always present solutions to decision-makers, rather than just critiques.

Identify that it is ultimately outside your control the extent to which others consult with you on a given decision, and the success and failure that comes from those decisions is not your responsibility if you have made a reasonable attempt to communicate your informed contribution to the

Lack of communication with stakeholders regarding changes

Potential individuals' symptoms

Feelings of resentment towards those perceived as making decisions or changes without communication.

A sense of ineffectiveness.

Task procrastination.

Lower productivity.

Anxiety of not being able to complete the task to own/others perceived levels of requirements.

Organisation preventions/remedies

Consult with the individual about the extent to which they feel they need additional information about upcoming changes.

Communicate changes to stakeholders, being respectful of the individual's knowledge, skills, and experience, with transparency around the how, what, when, where and why of the changes.

Ensure all information regarding changes is recorded in written documents that are reasonably accessible, convenient, and readable, along with the contact of the relevant stakeholder who can clarify information or answer any questions.

Individual preventions/remedies
Communicate information issues to your supervisor or human resource support.
Clearly and respectfully communicate your need for more information on given changes, staying in the context of how it would affect your own clearly defined tasks, roles and responsibilities and the organisation's goals.
Identify that it is ultimately outside your control the extent to which others give you information regarding changes, and the success and failure that comes from the availability of information is not your responsibility if you have made a reasonable attempt to request the information you feel is necessary.

Lack of support/training to help stakeholders through changes

Potential individuals' symptoms
Anxiety about judgements from other people.
A sense of ineffectiveness.
Task procrastination.
Lower productivity.
Anxiety of not being able to complete the task to own/others perceived levels of requirements.

Organisation preventions/remedies
Consult with the individual about what specific training
or support they feel they need to feel confident about
upcoming changes.
Identify tasks or responsibilities that can be paused or
delegated away from the individual to give them time
resources to undertake the necessary training or processing
time to optimally integrate the changes.

Individual preventions/remedies
Communicate current support issues, or projected future
support issues, to your supervisor or human resource
support in the context of how the changes will affect your
clearly defined tasks and roles.
Identify that a lack of support or training on a change may
not be from a lack of respect, but rather the decision maker's
lack of knowledge or oversight on how the changes will
impact your clearly defined tasks, roles, and responsibilities.
Identify that it is ultimately outside your control the extent to
which you are provided support or training for give changes,
and the success and failure that comes from those changes
is not your responsibility if you have made a reasonable
attempt to communicate your need for support and training
to the decision-makers.

Lack of listening to stakeholders

Potential individuals' symptoms
Feelings of resentment towards those perceived as
not listening.
Feelings of isolation.
A sense of inefficacy.

Reduced confidence.

Mentally exhausted due to certain issues not being resolved.

Organisation preventions/remedies

Identify and communicate the appropriate channels for the individual to share their thoughts in a way in which they will not be judged.

Periodically consult with the individual where they can express, without judgement, their thoughts. This should be followed up in a timely manner with a list of action/thought items that are communicated back to the individual for continuing discussions to speak to.

Consult with the individual for support that they do find listens well and consider how the individual may work together with that support for solutions to given issues.

Individual preventions/remedies

Identify alternative avenues of support who will unjudgementally listen than those at work (e.g., a trusted friend, family member or even formal counselling).

Communicate issues where you feel you are not being heard, with your supervisor or human resource support.

Consider a different approach or method of communication, identifying that different people have different preferred styles and methods of communication.

Emotionally mutually support others who are facing similar issues of not being heard.

Keep records of communications that can be talked to if conflicts arise.

Identify that it is ultimately outside your control the extent to which a given person listens to you. If you have made a reasonable attempt to communicate with the other party and you feel they do not listen, it may be a result of their own lack of training, knowledge and experience of their clearly defined roles and responsibilities.

Lack of clear feedback

Potential individuals' symptoms
Feelings of resentment towards those perceived as not providing clear feedback.
Anxiety about judgements from other people.
Anxiety of not being able to complete the task to own/others perceived levels of requirements.
Reduced confidence.
Task procrastination.
Lower productivity.
Mentally exhausted due to concentration and guessing.

Organisation preventions/remedies
Clearly consult the individual on their expectations for the amount of feedback that they will receive.
Consult with the individual for the methods they feel they best received feedback (in addition to written feedback)
Deliver feedback in a written format for which further conversations can refer to.
Identify the level of feedback required, considering the knowledge, skills, and experience of the individual.
Identify that feedback that is clear to one stakeholder may not be clear to another. Provide feedback to the lowest common denominator.

After giving feedback, communicate a convenient avenue or contact for which the individual can, without judgement, seek clarification.

Individual preventions/remedies
Communicate issues where you feel feedback is unclear, with your supervisor or human resource support.

Identify whether your own expectations of feedback align with that of the stakeholder providing feedback. You may come from different experiences of what the 'reasonable' amount of feedback is that is required for a given situation. Approach clarification on feedback by directly addressing feedback that you feel is not clear and providing your interpretation of the feedback for the other stakeholder to confirm or deny.

Identify that the extent to which you are given feedback is ultimately outside your control. If you have made a reasonable attempt to clarify feedback with the other party, it may be a result of their own lack of training, knowledge and experience of their clearly defined roles and responsibilities when it comes to providing you feedback.

Infrequent/lack of time-sensitive feedback

Potential individuals' symptoms
Feelings of resentment towards those perceived as not providing timely feedback.

Anxiety about judgements from other people.

Anxiety of not being able to complete the task to own/others perceived levels of requirements.

Reduced confidence.

Task procrastination.

Lower productivity.

Mentally exhausted due to concentration and guessing.

Organisation preventions/remedies

Clearly consult the individual on their expectations when and how much feedback they will receive.

Clearly set the expectations with the individual for when they will receive the feedback.

Provide additional training and support to those who are required to give timely feedback to help them deal with fluctuating demands (e.g., project management).

Identify the level of feedback required, considering the knowledge, skills, and experience of the individual.

Identify that feedback that is considered timely to one stakeholder may not be considered to another. Discuss this in the context of the priorities of the organisation's goals and the clearly defined tasks, roles, and responsibilities of each party.

Provide an avenue of timely support (e.g., peers) the individual can seek in the case where formal feedback is delayed.

Individual preventions/remedies

When submitting for feedback, communicate the priority of the feedback for your clearly defined tasks, roles, and responsibilities, and make a clear request for an expected time and date for the feedback. Take the initiative to communicate this with the stakeholder (e.g., setting a feedback meeting).

Consult with them as to their preferred methods of giving feedback to reduce their barriers to providing you feedback.

Communicate issues where you feel feedback is not
been given the correct frequency or timeliness with your
supervisor or human resource support. Always discuss in line
with your clearly defined tasks, roles, responsibilities, and
the organisation's goals.

Identify that the extent to which you are given feedback
is ultimately outside your control. If you have made a
reasonable attempt to get timely feedback from the other
party, it may be a result of their own lack of training,
knowledge and experience of their clearly defined roles and
responsibilities when it comes to providing you feedback.

Unfair negative feedback

Potential individuals' symptoms
Feelings of resentment towards those perceived as giving
unfair feedback.

Anxiety about judgements from other people.

Reduced confidence.

Task procrastination.

Lower productivity.

Sense of isolation.

Organisation preventions/remedies
If there are issues identified in a result, consult with the
individual to identify the reason behind the outcome, rather
than just focus on the outcome.

Consult with the individual on the feedback they have
received if they feel any of it was unfair or misinformed.
Identify that the individual's results may have been caused
by issues beyond their control and not malicious intent.

Identify that the individual's results may have been the result of a lack of training, and not malicious intent.

Individual preventions/remedies
Communicate with the feedback provider why you felt the feedback was unfair by providing the circumstances and inputs that led to the results.

Identify that different people have different knowledge, skills, and experiences when it comes to giving feedback, and they might lack in the ability to communicate constructive feedback in a way that is not perceived as negative. Discuss this issue with your supervisor or human resources support.

Identify that your sense of accomplishment or failure should not be dependent on the feedback or opinions of others, but rather your own sense of achievement.

Seek emotional support (informal or formal) if you feel you are unable to process another person's feedback without taking it personally.

Practice mindfulness to help you rest from processing feedback.

Lack of trust

Potential individuals' symptoms
Feelings of resentment towards those perceived as not trusting.

Anxiety about judgements from other people.

Reduced confidence.

Sense of isolation.

Lower productivity.

A sense of inefficacy.

Organisation preventions/remedies
Clearly define and communicate an individual's role, tasks, and responsibilities to all relevant stakeholders. Identify who is clearly defined as holding the responsibility for the outcome of the task or role and communicate the importance of autonomy to other stakeholders.

Provide a channel where individuals, without judgement, can communicate where they feel untrusted to complete their clearly defined responsibilities.

If an individual is believed to not be fulfilling their clearly defined responsibilities, communicate this to the individual along with clear evidence and a training path forward or the withdrawal of the individual from those responsibilities. This should be immediately followed by giving them responsibilities for which they have the appropriate knowledge, skills, or experience.

Individual preventions/remedies

Clearly communicate with supervision or human resource support the areas where you feel there is a lack of trust in your clearly defined responsibilities.

Identify that other people have different knowledge and experiences, and their lack of trust in your abilities is not necessarily a reflection of your knowledge, skills, and experience.

Identify if the mistrust is a miscommunication, misunderstanding or something for which there is evidence and consult the individual on whether you need to change a method for a task that is their clearly defined responsibility, or they need to allow you to complete the task or role in the way you see fit given it is your clearly defined responsibility.

Cliques of stakeholders

Potential individuals' symptoms

Anxiety about judgements from other people.

Reduced confidence.

Sense of isolation.

Preoccupation with impressing others.

Organisation preventions/remedies

Create a culture where there are crossover tasks requiring participation between different departments and groups of workers.

Create tasks that rotate between pairs of people (e.g., client presentations, strategic planning)

Consult with the individual about what environment they feel they work best in.

Individual preventions/remedies

Identify that different people come from different life experiences and may naturally group together with people who are perceived to have commonalities. The best way to identify commonalities with others is to engage with them in conversation. The best way to engage with others in conversation is when completing a task together.

Discuss with the other people/person and your supervisor what tasks you could be grouped together to complete.

In conflict with supervision/management

Potential individuals' symptoms

Reduced confidence.

Sense of isolation.

Anxiety about judgements from other people.

A sense of inefficacy.

Anxiety about future career prospects.

Physical exhaustion.

Anxiety about going to work or interacting with the supervisor/manager.

Organisation preventions/remedies

Provide a channel where individuals, without judgement, can communicate where they feel there is conflict present and would like to pursue mediation support.

Provide training to supervision and management on conflict management.

Consult with the individual and supervision in conflict and identify exactly whose responsibilities the task or role in question falls under. If the tasks and roles have not already been clearly defined, now is the time to do so, so that all discussions can be talked about in the context of tasks, roles, and responsibilities.

Individual preventions/remedies
Identify that other people have different knowledge and experiences, and a conflict over an issue is not necessarily a reflection of your knowledge, skills, and experience.
Always discuss issues with the other person by talking exactly to the clearly defined roles, tasks, and responsibilities of both parties.
Always discuss conflicts using "I feel..." and "It is my understanding..." rather than "You..." language.
Identify if the conflict is a miscommunication or misunderstanding.
Pursue resources for increasing your skills and training in conflict management and resolution.
Pursue mediation resources from human resources support.
Practice mindfulness to help you rest from processing the conflict.
Seek emotional support (informal or formal) if you feel you are unable to process the conflict.
Keep records of communications that can be talked to in mediation.

In conflict with co-workers

Potential individuals' symptoms
Reduced confidence.

Sense of isolation.

Anxiety about judgements from other people.

A sense of inefficacy.

Anxiety about future career prospects.

Physical exhaustion.

Anxiety about going to work or interacting with
the co-worker.

Organisation preventions/remedies

Provide a channel where individuals, without judgement, can
communicate where they feel there is conflict present and
would like to pursue mediation support.

Provide training to individuals on conflict management.
Consult with the individuals in conflict and identify exactly
whose responsibilities the task or role in question falls under.
If the tasks and roles have not already been clearly defined,
now is the time to do so, so that all discussions have been
talked exactly to these.

Provide mediation for co-workers if the conflict is over a
responsibility. If the conflict is over differences of approach,
provide guidance for the best course of action, in the context
of the organisation's goals.

Individual preventions/remedies

Identify that other people have different knowledge and
experiences, and a conflict over an issue is not necessarily a
reflection of your knowledge, skills, and experience.
Always discuss issues with the other person by talking
exactly to the clearly defined roles, tasks, and responsibilities
of both parties.

Always discuss conflicts using "I feel..." and "It is my understanding..." rather than "You..." language.
Identify if the conflict is a miscommunication or misunderstanding.
Pursue resources for increasing your skills and training in conflict management and resolution.
Pursue mediation from supervision or human resources support.
Practice mindfulness to help you rest from processing the conflict.
Seek emotional support (informal or formal) if you feel you are unable to process the conflict.
Keep records of communications that can be talked to in mediation.

Differences in cultural fits

Potential individuals' symptoms
Sense of isolation.

Anxiety about judgements from other people.
Anxiety about going to work or interacting with the co-worker.

Organisation preventions/remedies
Provide training and guidance to workers on diversity and inclusivity.
Consult with individuals about any barriers they feel are present for fitting in with the workplace culture.
Consult with the individual about what environment they feel they work best in.

Set the expectations with individuals very early for what the typical workplace culture is by providing examples of activities and tasks that take place throughout the year.

Individual preventions/remedies
Identify that you ultimately have control over what you say and do in the workplace, and you do not have to pursue or partake in cultures that you feel conflict with your own.
Pursue assertiveness training to learn to respectfully express your feelings and needs.
Identify what personal needs you are seeking to gain from the culture at work and consider if there may be alternative sources that could fulfil those needs (e.g., friends outside of work, sports club, church)

Solitary work

Potential individuals' symptoms
Sense of isolation.

Reduced confidence.

Anxiety about future career prospects.

A sense of inefficacy.

Mental exhaustion from guessing courses of action.

Organisation preventions/remedies
Provide opportunities for the individual to take place in group activities (e.g., networking, group tasks, buddy tasks).
Provide them with channels of periodic communication to supervision, mentor, or peer support.
Consult with the individual on the extent to which they would like periodic feedback and check-ins.

Individual preventions/remedies

Identify what personal needs you are seeking to gain from work and consider if there may be alternative sources that could fulfil those needs (e.g., friends outside of work, sports club, church)

Maintain a healthy social life by instigating and taking part in social activities that align with your interests.

Consider which tasks of your work could be done in partnership with another stakeholder (e.g., travel, lunch or talking through ideas).

Required to work in a location with a lack of facilities

Potential individuals' symptoms

Feelings of resentment towards those setting work tasks.

Physical exhaustion.

Mental exhaustion due to increased decision-making.

Sense of isolation.

Perceived lack of care.

Organisation preventions/remedies

Periodically consult with individuals' facility issues that they believe exist now, or may exist in the future, for them completing their tasks.

Consult with the individual about the support, resources or training required to continue their given tasks.

Provide the appropriate support and resources for individuals to be able to optimally complete their roles and tasks.

Set the expectations with individuals very early for what they can expect in terms of facilities as they fulfil their tasks and role.

Individual preventions/remedies
Communicate facility issues as soon as they are apparent, or perceived to be coming, with your supervisor, along with proposed solutions that fit with the goals of the organisation. Identify that facility issues may not necessarily be caused by the decisions of one individual, but rather may be the result of a systematic organisational issue.
Identify that resource availability is likely dependent on a wide scope of factors that are ultimately outside your control. If you have made a reasonable effort to pursue decreasing the access barriers, but they remain, consider that your success or failures for the given tasks is not your ultimate responsibility, but that of the organisation.

Required to frequently travel

Potential individuals' symptoms
Sense of isolation.
Physical exhaustion due to unable to conveniently follow healthy habits.
Mental exhaustion due to increased decision-making.
A lack of work/life balance.
Anxiety over meeting requirements while in unfamiliar settings.

Organisation preventions/remedies
Provide the appropriate support and resources for
individuals to be able to optimally complete their roles
and tasks.
Provide support and training for pre-planning as much as
possible. Delegate jobs away as much as possible.
Set the expectations with individuals very early for what they
can expect in terms of the amount of travel required to fulfil
their tasks and role.

Individual preventions/remedies
Identify which healthy habits you can pursue while travelling
(e.g., finding time for physical exercise)
Pre-plan break activities and practice mindfulness to help
you rest from work.
Identify channels you can use to stay connected with friends
and family during travel.
Try different methods for achieving healthy habits (e.g., for
sleep, try sleeping masks and ear plugs).
Seek support from your organisation to delegate appropriate
tasks away.
Seek resources from your organisation to make your travel
more comfortable.

Working in a distracting environment

Potential individuals' symptoms
Feelings of resentment towards those who are perceived to
have created the environment.
Mentally exhausted due to focus.

Anxiety of not being able to complete the task to own/others perceived levels of requirements.

Task procrastination.

Perceived lack of care.

Organisation preventions/remedies
Consult with the individual about the environment they require to complete their tasks and role.

Consult with the individual about the resources (e.g., headphones) they require to complete their tasks and role in comfort.

Identify the extent to which providing an individual with a less distracting environment would align with the organisation's goals.

Regularly consult with the individual about any environment current issues, or perceived upcoming issues.

Individual preventions/remedies
Communicate environmental issues as soon as they are apparent, or perceived to be coming, with your supervisor, along with proposed solutions that fit with the goals of the organisation.

If the distraction is other people's behaviours, respectfully but assertively communicate the issue to them and ask them to adjust their behaviours so that you can more optimally complete your clearly defined responsibilities.

Request support or resources to help you complete your tasks and role in an increased level of comfort.

Bullying (including behaviours that cause individuals distress, harm, or intimidation)

Potential individuals' symptoms

Sense of isolation.

Anxiety about judgements from other people.
Anxiety about going to work or interacting with
the co-worker.

Reduced confidence.

Mental exhaustion from being unable to focus.

Physical exhaustion.

Preoccupation with thinking about the bullying, distracting
from work and lower productivity.

Organisation preventions/remedies

Provide support and training to help individuals identify
bullying behaviours.

Provide secure channels of communication for bullying to be
reported, both for the victim and any witnesses.

Have clear policies and expectations of workplace
behaviours, including those of third-party stakeholders
such as customers and suppliers, using documentation
and signage.

Conduct periodic behavioural reviews for
systematic problems.

Provide individuals with support (e.g., counselling) and
resources (e.g., mental health day) after an incident. Always
confidentially follow up on incidents with the victim so they
feel heard and cared for.

Introduce reasonable means of security as deterrents of
incidents (e.g., security personnel, cameras).

Individual preventions/remedies

Communicate issues of bullying as soon as they are apparent, or perceived to be coming, with your supervisor, human resources support, a trusted colleague or advisor who can guide you through the steps to make a formal complaint to the organisation.

Keep a record of all interactions/incidents with the perpetrator that may be used for the purposes of an investigation.

Identify that bullying of any kind is not okay, regardless of how normal or systemic others in the workplace make it seem.

If you feel comfortable, communicate with the bully how their behaviours make you feel and ask them to stop.

Seek emotional support (informal or formal).

Maintain a healthy social life by instigating and taking part in social activities with trusted friends and family.

Practice mindfulness to help you rest from processing the bullying.

Harassment (including discrimination based on individuals' characteristics such as gender, race, age, religion etc.)

Potential individuals' symptoms

Sense of isolation.

Anxiety about judgements from other people.

Anxiety about going to work or interacting with the co-worker.

Reduced confidence.

Mental exhaustion from being unable to focus.

Physical exhaustion.
Preoccupation with thinking about the harassment, distracting from work and lower productivity.

Organisation preventions/remedies
Provide support and training to help individuals identify harassment.
Provide secure channels of communication for harassment to be reported, both for the victim or any witnesses.
Have clear policies and expectations of workplace behaviours, including those of third-party stakeholders such as customers and suppliers, using documentation and signage.
Conduct periodic behavioural reviews for systematic problems.
Provide individuals with support (e.g., counselling, legal advisory) and resources (e.g., mental health day) after an incident. Always confidentially follow up on incidents with the victim so they feel heard and cared for.

Individual preventions/remedies
Communicate issues of bullying as soon as they are apparent, or perceived to be coming, with your supervisor, human resources support, a trusted colleague or advisor who can guide you through the steps to make a formal complaint to the organisation.
Keep a record of all interactions/incidents with the perpetrator that may be used for the purposes of an investigation.
Identify that harassment of any kind is not okay, regardless of how normal or systemic others in the workplace make it seem.

Seek emotional support (informal or formal).
If you feel the harassment is not appropriately addressed, seek legal advice.
Maintain a healthy social life by instigating and taking part in social activities with trusted friends and family.
Practice mindfulness to help you rest from processing the harassment.

Threatening Behaviours

Potential individuals' symptoms
Anxiety about going to work or interacting with the stakeholder category (e.g., customer, co-worker)
Reduced confidence.
Mental exhaustion from being unable to focus.
Preoccupation with thinking about the threat, distracting from work and lower productivity.

Organisation preventions/remedies
Provide support and training to help individuals identify threatening behaviour.
Provide secure channels of communication for threats to be reported, both for the victim and any witnesses.
Have clear policies and expectations of workplace behaviours, including those of third-party stakeholders such as customers and suppliers, using documentation and signage.
Conduct periodic behavioural reviews for systematic problems.

Provide individuals with support (e.g., counselling) and resources (e.g., mental health day) after an incident. Always confidentially follow up on incidents with the victim so they feel heard and cared for.

Introduce reasonable means of security as deterrents of incidents (e.g., security personnel, cameras).

Individual preventions/remedies
Communicate an incident straight away with your supervisor, human resources support, a trusted colleague or advisor who can guide you through the steps to make a formal complaint to the organisation.

Keep a record of the incident that may be used for the purposes of an investigation.

Identify that bullying of any kind is not okay, regardless of how normal or systemic others in the workplace make it seem.

If you feel comfortable, communicate with the bully how their behaviours make you feel and ask them to stop.

Seek emotional support (informal or formal).

Maintain a healthy social life by instigating and taking part in social activities with trusted friends and family.

Practice mindfulness to help you rest from processing the incident.

Communicate with supervisors what resources or support (e.g., surveillance, security personnel) you feel is reasonable to cope with any systematic issues of threatening behaviour.

Gossip

Potential individuals' symptoms
Sense of isolation.

Anxiety about judgements from other people.

Reduced confidence.

Mental exhaustion from being unable to focus.
Preoccupation with thinking about the opinions of others, distracting from work and lower productivity.

Increased cynicism about others' behaviours and attitudes.

Organisation preventions/remedies
Encourage a culture through leadership setting examples, where topics are only discussed where they are directly relevant to an individual's clearly defined tasks, roles, and responsibilities.

Provide secure channels of communication for gossip to be reported, both for the victim or any witnesses.

Have clear policies and expectations of workplace behaviours, including those of third-party stakeholders such as customers and suppliers, using documentation and signage.

Individual preventions/remedies
Communicate issues of gossip as soon as they are apparent with your supervisor, human resources support, a trusted colleague or advisor who can guide you through the steps to make a formal complaint to the organisation.

If you feel comfortable, communicate with the gossiping person how their behaviours make you feel and ask them to stop.

Identify that gossip is not okay, regardless of how normal or systemic others in the workplace make it seem.

Seek emotional support (informal or formal).

Maintain a healthy social life by instigating and taking part in social activities with trusted friends and family.
Practice mindfulness to help you rest from processing any gossip incidents.
Encourage a culture by setting an example, where you only discuss topics that are directly relevant to another individual's clearly defined tasks, roles, and responsibilities.

Exposure to unstable people

Potential individuals' symptoms
Anxiety about going to work or interacting with others.
Reduced confidence.
Mental exhaustion from increased decision-making.
Physical exhaustion from being tense.
Sense of isolation.

Organisation preventions/remedies
Provide support and training to help individuals identify high-risk behavioural cues and respond to incidents.
Provide secure channels of communication for threats/harassment to be reported, both for the victim or any witnesses.
Have clear policies and expectations of workplace behaviours, including those of third-party stakeholders such as clients, using documentation and signage.
Conduct periodic behavioural reviews for systematic problems.

Provide individuals with support (e.g., counselling) and resources (e.g., mental health day) after an incident. Always confidentially follow up on incidents with the victim so they feel heard and cared for.

Introduce reasonable means of security as deterrents of incidents (e.g., security personnel, cameras).

Set the expectations with individuals very early for what they can expect in terms of interactions as they fulfil their tasks and role.

Individual preventions/remedies
Identify that most people you are dealing with are people who need help, even if they are unable/unwilling to express it.

Pursue training on having emotional detachment from people so you can focus on solutions.

Undertake any support and resources offered by the organisation after an incident. You don't have to prove to anyone how tough you are.

Pursue support and training to help you identify high-risk behavioural cues and respond to incidents with your own safety as a priority.

Practice mindfulness to help you rest from processing incidents.

Physically and emotionally mutually support co-workers who are set with the same tasks.

Highly competitive environment

Potential individuals' symptoms
Feelings of resentment towards supervision for creating a competitive environment.

Feelings of isolation.

Anxiety of being compared to others.

Anxiety of being discussed behind one's back.

Mental exhaustion from increased efforts.

Physical exhaustion from increased efforts.

Organisation preventions/remedies
Identify the extent the goals of the organisation are exceeded by creating a highly competitive environment.
Clearly define each individual's roles and tasks and the possible directions of their career progressions.
Set expectations early for career progression opportunities by clearly defining the criteria for obtaining projects/promotions.
Encourage and promote recognition for team achievements, rather than just individual achievements.

Individual preventions/remedies
Identify that your successes and failures should not be compared to others but only to what you can achieve given your prior training, knowledge, and experience. You don't need to prove anything to anyone.

Practice mindfulness to help you rest from anxieties.
Clearly communicate with supervision if you do not understand the available career progression opportunities.
Seek out training and professional development opportunities to upskill towards your career goals.
Pursue short-term activities that help fulfil some of your work desires (e.g., volunteer in a charity or sports organisation).

Questionable/Unethical work practices

Potential individuals' symptoms
Feelings of isolation.
Anxiety of being discussed behind one's back.
Mental exhaustion from processing guilt/shame
and confusion.
Physical exhaustion.
Anxiety about future life prospects.
Anxiety about future career prospects.
Increased cynicism about others' behaviours and attitudes.

Organisation preventions/remedies
Set the expectations with individuals very early for what they
can expect in terms of practices as they fulfil their tasks and
role and consult if they find personal objections to the tasks.
Have clear policies and expectations of workplace practices,
including those of third-party stakeholders such as clients,
using documentation and signage.
Provide secure channels of communication for questionable/
unethical work practices to be reported.
Regularly consult, without judgement, with the individual for
their perceptions of work practices.

Individual preventions/remedies
Identify that other people have different knowledge and
experiences, and a conflict over the ethicality of a work
practice does not necessarily mean the practice is wrong. You
do, however, ultimately have the choice over whether you
participate in the practice.

Clearly communicate and hold to any boundaries you have on work practices.
If you are unsure of the legality of a work practice, seek legal advice.

Lack of work-life balance

Potential individuals' symptoms
Mental exhaustion from overwork.
Physical exhaustion from overwork or lack of healthy choices.
Social isolation.
Self-resentment of guilt or shame for neglecting life or work.
Reduced productivity.

Organisation preventions/remedies
Have clear policies and expectations of workplace practices and boundaries, using documentation, signage, and training.
Have leadership lead by example by having boundaries of time spent in work and life.
Periodically consult, without judgement, with individuals for their work practices and boundaries and the extent they feel they are in control.

Individual preventions/remedies
Clearly communicate your work boundaries to all other stakeholders. Identify that their reactions to your boundaries come from their own knowledge, experiences, and personal views, but this does not mean you need to change your boundaries in line with their reactions. You do not need to prove anything to anyone.

Maintain a healthy social life by instigating and taking part in social activities with trusted friends and family.
Practice mindfulness to help you rest from processing any gossip incidents.

Lack of social support

Potential individuals' symptoms
Social isolation.
Self-resentment of guilt or shame for neglecting life or work.
Reduced confidence.
Anxiety of being discussed behind one's back.
Increased cynicism about others' behaviours and attitudes.

Organisation preventions/remedies
Provide opportunities for the individual to take place in group activities (e.g., networking, group tasks, buddy tasks).
Provide them with channels of periodic communication to supervision, mentor, or peer support.
Create a culture where there are crossover tasks requiring participation between different departments and groups of workers.
Create tasks that rotate between pairs of people (e.g., client presentations, strategic planning)

Individual preventions/remedies
Initiate/maintain a healthy social life by instigating and taking part in social activities with family, groups and organisations that share similar interests (e.g., sporting

groups, church). Identify that people change over time, and although there may not have been a connection at a previous point in time, mutual support may be possible after re-making contact.

Pursue formal counselling if you feel you have difficulty connecting with others.

Practice mindfulness to help you rest from processing anxiety or guilt.

Identify that social rejection is not necessarily a reflection on you or your personality, but rather may have been a result of a lack of connection with that other individual. Past social rejection does not guarantee future social rejection.

Unreasonably high personal expectations

Potential individuals' symptoms
Self-resentment of guilt or shame for previous choices.

Anxiety of being compared to others.

Anxiety of being discussed behind one's back.

Mental exhaustion from increased efforts.

Physical exhaustion from increased efforts.

Social isolation.

Distracting preoccupation with achievements.

Anxiety about future life prospects.

Anxiety about future career prospects.

Organisation preventions/remedies
Clearly define to the individual their roles and tasks and consult with the individual for what should be the reasonable expectations of achievements for a given time period.

Ensure that stakeholders are not contributing to the individual's high expectations by clearly communicating the reasonable expectations for their achievements.
Ensure the organisation is not contributing to the individual's high expectations by having adequate resources and support for the individual to fulfil their tasks and roles.
Recognise the individual's achievements or contributions to the organisation's goals, rather than just traditional milestones.

Individual preventions/remedies
Identify that your successes and failures are always contributed to by factors beyond your control. They are not necessarily a reflection of your skills, knowledge, or experience.
Seek informal emotional or formal mental health support if you feel you are unable to process the extent to which your expectations and performance are different.
Initiate/maintain a healthy work-life balance by instigating and taking part in social activities with family, groups and organisations that share similar interests (e.g., sporting groups, church).
Identify when you have made any achievement, large or small, and celebrate each achievement, rather than always waiting for a future achievement to come to fruition.

Recognition, reward and fair treatment

Lack of perceived value in work

Potential individuals' symptoms

Cynical about work value.

Anxiety about future life prospects.

Distracting preoccupation with other activities.

Reduced productivity.

Task procrastination.

Anxiety of being compared to others.

Anxiety of being discussed behind one's back.

Organisation preventions/remedies

Clearly communicate to all stakeholders the positive impact that the organisation is having on other stakeholders.
Clearly communicate to the individual how their clearly defined roles and tasks contribute to the organisation's goals.
Set expectations early of the organisations' goals and how it impacts other individuals or organisations.
Consult with the individual for if there are organisational tasks they perceive as higher value and identify if there are opportunities for the individual to contribute to that area.

Individual preventions/remedies

Identify that there are often tasks that need to get done that contribute inherent value to another role or task. If you are unable to identify the value of a task, clearly communicate this to supervision.

Identify if there are other roles and tasks in the organisation you feel are of higher value and consult with your supervisor for if there are opportunities for you to contribute to that area.

Identify that the value of your work is restricted by what you can achieve given the scope of your task, role, or responsibilities. If you feel the scope of your work could be expanded to have higher value, communicate this to your supervisor.

Pursue short-term activities that help fulfil the values you feel are lacking in your role (e.g., volunteer in a charity).

Lack of rewards for work (e.g., perceivably fair compensation or bonuses)

Potential individuals' symptoms
Feelings of resentment towards supervision/leadership for lack of rewards.

Anxiety about future life prospects.

Reduced productivity.

Task procrastination.

A distracting preoccupation with careers (e.g., job searching) or money.

Cynical about work value.

Organisation preventions/remedies
Set expectations early in concrete terms for what compensation or bonuses are available in the role and how they will be activated. Consult early with the individual about if there is a perceived lack of fairness to these milestones. Ensure there is parity compensation between individuals with comparable skills, knowledge, and experience.

Consult with the individual for if they believe there has been a compensatory oversight. Provide transparent justification for how the individual's compensation is set in line with the organisation's goals.

Consult, respectfully and without judgement, if they would like independent financial counselling resources or support, identifying that people's knowledge of financially responsible practices and priorities likely differ from your own.

Individual preventions/remedies
Identify that your rewards were likely set in line with the organisation's goals and priorities and is not necessarily an accurate representation of your knowledge, skills, or experience.

Practice mindfulness to help you rest from anxieties. Clearly communicate with supervision if you do not understand the justification for the available rewards. Clearly communicate with supervision if you feel your rewards were made under misunderstanding or miscommunication of your role or tasks, providing evidence for fairer compensation.

Seek out training and professional development opportunities to upskill towards your compensation goal, as long as these are known to be in line with organisational goals.

Pursue financial counselling if you feel your life expenditures are not being met by your compensation.

No recognition for achievements

Potential individuals' symptoms
Feelings of resentment towards supervision/leadership for lack of recognition.

Anxiety of being compared to others.

Reduced productivity.

Task procrastination.

A distracting preoccupation with careers (e.g., job searching) or achievements.

Cynical about work value.

Organisation preventions/remedies
Recognise individual achievements of contributions to the organisation's goals, rather than just traditional milestones.
Encourage and promote recognition for team achievements, in addition to individual achievements.
Recognise an individual's achievements publicly, rather than just to the individual.

Individual preventions/remedies
Identify that your recognised achievements are not necessarily an accurate representation of your knowledge, skills, or experience.
Identify each of your own achievements, large or small, and celebrate each achievement.
Identify that a lack of achievement recognition may be from a lack of miscommunication or misunderstanding. If you believe this is the case, communicate your achievements to your supervisor, in the context of how it relates to your tasks, roles and organisational goals.

Biased treatment of stakeholders

Potential individuals' symptoms
Feelings of resentment towards supervision/leadership for
unfair treatment
Anxiety of being compared to others.
A distracting preoccupation with others' work
and achievements.
Anxiety of being discussed behind one's back.
Social isolation.
Anxiety about future career prospects.

Organisation preventions/remedies
Clearly define to the individual their roles and tasks and
consult with the individual for what should be the reasonable
expectations of achievements for a given time period.
Encourage and promote recognition for team achievements,
rather than just individual achievements.
Provide justifications (where it is not in breach of
appropriate confidentiality) for the abnormal treatment of
one individual over another.
Where reasonable, have a stakeholder's abnormal treatment
be decided by a committee rather than an individual.

Individual preventions/remedies
Identify that other stakeholders have their own motivations
and goals, and those motivations may be at odds with
your own goals. You are ultimately not responsible for the
behaviours of other people; you can only influence them.

Clearly communicate with your supervisor or human resources support if you feel that the treatment someone else received should also be applied to you, providing evidence to support your case.

Lack of recognition of abilities

Potential individuals' symptoms
Feelings of resentment towards supervision/leadership for lack of recognition.
Anxiety of being compared unfairly to others.
A distracting preoccupation with being recognised.
Mental exhaustion from increased efforts.
Physical exhaustion from increased efforts.

Organisation preventions/remedies
Clearly define to the individual their roles and tasks and consult with the individual for what should be the reasonable expectations of achievements for a given time period, in line with their abilities.
Recognise the individual's achievements of contributions to the organisation's goals, rather than just traditional milestones.

Individual preventions/remedies
Identify that your recognised abilities are not necessarily an accurate representation of your knowledge, skills, or experience.
Identify each of your own achievements, large or small, and celebrate each achievement as a reflection of your abilities.

Identify that a lack of ability recognition may be from a lack of miscommunication or misunderstanding. If you believe this is the case, communicate your achievements to your supervisor, in the context of how it relates to your abilities contributed towards the organisational goals.

Biased policies and procedures

Potential individuals' symptoms
Feelings of resentment towards supervision/leadership for unfair treatment.
A distracting preoccupation with others' work and achievements.
Anxiety of being discussed behind one's back.
Social isolation.
Anxiety about future career prospects.

Organisation preventions/remedies
Provide justifications (where it is not in breach of appropriate confidentiality) for the abnormal treatment of one individual over another.
Where reasonable, have a stakeholder's abnormal treatment be decided by a committee rather than an individual.
Clearly document all policies and procedures in writing, in a conveniently accessible location that can be accessed by all relevant stakeholders for enquiry.
Ensure all stakeholders have the training and support for understanding the necessary policies and procedures.

Individual preventions/remedies
Identify that other stakeholders have their own motivations
and goals, and those motivations may be at odds with
your own goals. You are ultimately not responsible for the
behaviours of other people; you can only influence them.
Communicate issues of policy as soon as they are apparent
with your supervisor, human resources support, a trusted
colleague or advisor who can guide you through the steps to
make a formal complaint to the organisation.
If you feel the policy issue is not appropriately addressed,
seek legal advice.
Practice mindfulness to help you rest from processing
the issues.

Negative feedback for events beyond stakeholder's control

Potential individuals' symptoms
Feeling a sense of ineffectiveness.
Anxiety of not being able to complete the task to own/others
perceived levels of requirements.
Anxiety of discipline/reprimand/judgement for outcomes.
Task procrastination.

Organisation preventions/remedies
Provide the support and resources for stakeholders to
understand the extent to which individuals have control
over outcomes.
Consult with individuals where they feel there is a lack of
control over outcomes and reassure or correct individuals
as required.

If there are issues identified in a result, consult with the individual to identify the reason behind the outcome, rather than just focus on the outcome.

Consult with the individual on the feedback they have received and if they feel any of it was unfair or misinformed. If an event is found to be beyond the stakeholder's control, ask stakeholders to publicly apologise to the individual and request training for the stakeholder to better understand the individual's clearly defined role and tasks.

Individual preventions/remedies
Identify that the negative feedback may be from miscommunication or misunderstanding. If you believe this is the case, respectfully but clearly communicate the context and circumstances to your supervisor.

Identify that other stakeholders have their own perspectives, and those perspectives may be incorrect. You are ultimately not responsible for the perspectives of other people; you can only influence them.

Lack of addressing inappropriate behaviours

Potential individuals' symptoms
Feelings of resentment towards supervision/leadership for not addressing issues.

A distracting preoccupation with the stakeholder.

Cynicism of fair organisational justice.

Organisation preventions/remedies
Provide justifications (where it is not in breach of appropriate confidentiality) for the abnormal treatment of one individual over another.

Where reasonable, have a stakeholder's abnormal treatment be decided by a committee rather than an individual.

Clearly document all policies and procedures in writing, in a conveniently accessible location that can be accessed by all relevant stakeholders for enquiry.

Ensure all stakeholders have the training and support for understanding the necessary policies and procedures.

Provide a secure channel of communication for victims and witnesses to report perceived incidents where inappropriate treatment went unresolved.

Individual preventions/remedies
Identify that other people have different knowledge and experiences, and a disagreement over the extent to which a behaviour is addressed does not necessarily mean it was addressed inappropriately. You do, however, ultimately have the choice over whether you continue participation in the organisation.

Clearly communicate and hold to any boundaries you have on work practices.

Communicate issues of policy as soon as they are apparent with your supervisor, human resources support, a trusted colleague or advisor who can guide you through the steps to make a formal complaint to the organisation.

If you feel the policy issue is not appropriately addressed, seek legal advice.

Practice mindfulness to help you rest from processing the issues.

Lack of addressing stakeholder's individualised needs

Potential individuals' symptoms

Feelings of resentment towards unempathetic supervision.
Anxiety of not being able to complete the task to own/others perceived levels of requirements.
Anxiety of discipline/reprimand/judgement for outcomes.

Organisation preventions/remedies

Identify the sources of unempathetic support (remember, it might be you as well) and provide adequate training on how to provide empathetic, individualised support.
Periodically consult with the individual on what issues they are facing/needs they have.
Provide training, support and resources that can help individuals optimally achieve their tasks and roles, identifying that individuals have a diverse range of experience, skills, and knowledge.
Ensure all training, support and resources are accessible to all stakeholders, regardless of their accessibility needs.

Individual preventions/remedies

Communicate issues where you feel you are not being heard or empathised with, with your supervisor or human resource support. Where possible, provide solution options immediately after communicating the issue.
Emotionally mutually support others who are facing similar issues.

Lack of flexible policies

Potential individuals' symptoms
Feelings of resentment towards unempathetic supervision.
Anxiety of not being able to complete the task to own/others perceived levels of requirements.
Anxiety of discipline/reprimand/judgement for outcomes.

Organisation preventions/remedies
Clearly document all policies and procedures in writing, in a conveniently accessible location that all relevant stakeholders can access for enquiry.
Ensure all stakeholders have the training and support for understanding the necessary policies and procedures.
Allow supervisors to have transparent autonomy in how policies are applied. Ensure that any abnormal applications of a policy are clearly documented to ensure parity with other individuals should a similar situation arise in the future or an enquiry be made.

Individual preventions/remedies
Identify that organisational goals, which policies were aiming to meet, may be at odds with your own goals and personal values. You are ultimately not responsible for other people's behaviours; you can only influence them.
Clearly communicate and hold to any boundaries you have on work policies to your supervisor.
If you feel the policy issue is not appropriately addressed, seek legal advice.
Practice mindfulness to help you rest from processing the issues.

Acknowledgements

Firstly, thank you to my lovely wife Loren for your support and allowing me to embark on this adventure of helping others with stress and burnout. Additional thanks to Haddie and Jeremy for providing lots of love, giggles, and good distractions from work.

Thank you to all the clients, managers, supervisors, and mentors over the years who have granted me their wisdom regarding how they have personally and organisationally attempted to deal with burnout. A special thanks to Jan Easton for your business advisory and for being an example of a force of positivity and competence in the face of stressors.

Further Resources

For further diving into burnout, I strongly recommend *Burnout: A guide to identifying burnout and pathways to recovery (Taylor & Francis, 2022)*. The authors, Parker, Tavella and Eyers, have made serious strides in the understanding and knowledge of stress and burnout from those made in the late 20th century and are setting the new standard for burnout research.

For further reading of stress, I recommend *Principles and Practice of Stress Management (Guilford Publications, 2021)*. Although at times very heady and academic, it is a necessary refresher on many stress concepts and reduction methodologies.

For further practical resources, head to Coolout:

www.coolout.co

At Coolout, we help both organisations and individuals with stress management, burnout prevention and burnout recovery. We do this through education, courses, assessment and coaching. Come check out what we are doing!